Giving God What You Are

PAT BAKER

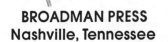

BROADMAN PRESS
Nashville, Tennessee

4253-33
ISBN: 0-8054-5333-4

Unless otherwise indicated Scripture verses are taken from
The Living Bible. Copyright © Tyndale House
Publishers, Wheaton, Illinois, 1971.
Used by permission.

Dewey Decimal Classification: 248.4
Subject heading: CHRISTIAN LIFE

Library of Congress Catalog Card Number: 80-69586
Printed in the United States of America

To my husband, Don
God has given him to me
to help fulfill the purpose
for my life

Acknowledgments

Rick Boland, proofreader
Kathy Boland, efficient typist
Jack Causey, gifted Bible story teller
The endless list of persons who
    allowed me to use
    portions of their
    life stories in this book
My family and friends who prayed me
    through this writing

Preface

Some of the biggest hurdles I must overcome as a Christian are believing, accepting, forgiving, and loving myself as God believes, accepts, forgives, and loves me. This truth is only one of the many truths I continue to learn about God as I pursue my Christian journey. I firmly believe in each new thing I learn about God. In each of these learning experiences, I ask him to help me incorporate them into my daily living.

This book is about the numerous ways Christians can come to know more about God. Some of these ways are painful, others are full of joy, and others simply come as an outgrowth of a desire to be totally submissive to God. Each of us learns to give God what common sense tells us we have to give. In this act God takes our offering and helps us develop our potentials for gradually becoming what he wants us to become through his Son.

Living our Christian lives through his Son is an important basic lesson with which we must come to grips. Paul discovered this along his journey, and he wrote: "I myself no longer live, but Christ lives in me. And the real life I now have within this body is a result of my trusting in the Son of God, who loved me and gave himself for me" (Gal. 2:20). I have learned that when I live my life through Jesus two things happen: I don't demand the impossible out of myself, and neither do I think that I have nothing to give back to God.

that I have nothing to give back to God.

When Christians commit themselves to walking toward the goals that God has for their lives, they will not waste precious time comparing their lives with other lives nor wishing that they were something that God never intended them to be. One of our greatest desires will be to become what he wants us to become.

This book offers suggestions to people who are wanting to find a deeper meaning in the continuation of their Christian lives. Somewhere during this pilgrimage there will come to those searching an unquenchable thirst to desire to live so closely with God that they will cry out to God from the depths of their souls, offering up to him all that they are.

So,

"Be happy

Grow in Christ . . . .

And may the God of love and peace be with you" (2 Cor. 13:11).

Contents

The Journey

I'm making a journey, Lord
The greatest journey of all
My steps may fail, Lord
So please don't let me fall

The way is narrow, Lord
And sometimes I feel alone
When my heart fears, Lord
I softly pray this song

Give me the heart to be pure
Give me the faith to be sure
Give me the strength to endure
All of my tribulations

I need some courage, Lord
To make it just one more mile
I want to hold your hand
I want to see you smile

Give me the heart to be pure
Give me the faith to be sure
Give me the strength to endure
All of my tribulations

Clawson/Courtney

It isn't sacrifices and offerings which you really want from your people. Burnt animals bring no special joy to your heart. But you have accepted the offer of my lifelong service. (Psalm 40:6)

1
Starting Your Life with God

Every person from the day of his physical birth has contact with God. There is another birth of which Jesus spoke, spiritual birth, the birth you experienced the moment you accepted him as your personal Savior.

When did you have this meeting with Jesus? Many years ago? Last week? Today? How much had you heard about him before you personally accepted him?

As a young child you had a minute comprehension of God. As you grew into older childhood, you gained a greater capacity for understanding spiritual truths. Possibly as an older child you had become acquainted with the concept of sin and the consequences of sin. Can you remember those painful times when you were punished by your parents for doing things they had told you not to do? An adult told about one of those times he remembered. As a small child, he had gone into a grocery store with an older boy and they stole some candy. The proprietor knew the young boy's father and called him about the episode. The father talked with his son about the incident and administered the consequences to the boy for the crime. The boy received a punishment because he had taken part in an act which involved stealing from another person — an act that was unacceptable to society.

That such an act is wrong is not difficult to learn at a very young age, but the concept of sinning against God is much harder to understand. It is usually during the elementary years that children gain the capacity for relating their lives to God. They hear words such as *saved, lost, sin, repent,* and *eternal life.* The word *eternal* begins to mean something important to that young life. It is something one can be sure of. It involves God's sacrifice and love, and it is something you can have. When you realize it can be yours, you want it. One day, all the knowledge you have about this personal relationship will culminate into a decision—your taking the first step toward accepting the gift of eternal life that God places into your hands through his Son, Jesus. You will never make a more important decision.

When I became a Christian, I can remember realizing that I loved Jesus. I wanted him to be my Savior, and I wanted to be his child. It was a very simple act of obedience to him at that early age. I have never forgotten the significance of that first personal meeting with Jesus.

I had so much to learn, but that was not an important factor at the time. I only knew I was happy with the decision I had made. I had started on my Christian journey with God. If I had been confronted at first with all that would be involved in being a Christian, it could have possibly overwhelmed me. Much later I was to realize that, from that first day as a new Christian, I would spend the rest of my life learning about God. Much later I was to realize that the more I would learn about him, the more of my life I would give to him. I felt at that first personal meeting I had given him all my life, at least as much of it as I knew how to give him then. I would learn through the opportunities God was going to give me to become better acquainted with this one who was now my personal guide.

Starting Your Life with God

How does a person learn to give God more of his life? How do you continue living in the world without letting the pulling influences of the world become your way of life? How do you know what is expected of your new life with Jesus?

First, you learn that Jesus can be your Savior, that he can help you conquer the power of sin in your life. But your acquaintance does not end there. You then get to know him as your Lord. You may need to borrow a Bible commentary, get a Bible dictionary, or whatever other books are necessary and study the word *Lord*. When you pray and use the word *Lord*, you must understand that you are going before the one who is now in control of your life. When you say "Lord," in essence you are saying, "I now come before you, believing that you are in control of my life. There are many things I can do, but help me understand that you will be in control of everything that will affect my life's purpose." With God being your Lord, you will never have to carry your responsibilities, your efforts, or your burdens alone.

> Then, knowing what lies ahead for you, you won't become bored with being a Christian, nor become spiritually dull and indifferent, but you will be anxious to follow the example of those who receive all that God has promised them because of their strong faith and patience (Heb. 6:12).

That is one of the purposes of this book, to encourage you to learn about and experience the excitement and the anticipation of growing in your life as a Christian. God says he wants you and me to "become mature in our understanding, as strong Christians ought to be" (Heb. 6:1). He wants us to learn what is involved in a personal relationship with him. We won't want to stop living long enough to ask if Christianity works, we know it works because it's happening right now in our lives.

A photographer had found a process of producing a colored picture with an unusually soft, delicate finish. When a nation-

15

ally acclaimed photography firm heard about this process, they said that it couldn't be done with the equipment he was using. They said that he would have had to replace his old equipment with the latest equipment available in order to produce the kind of picture he claimed to be producing. The photographer continued to disagree with them. Several representatives from the large firm were sent to check out the authenticity of the man's work. Even after they looked over the equipment and saw the finished product, they went away still saying, "It can't be done." There are people who hear how God can change lives. They see people's lives being transformed daily, and yet they are still saying, "It can't be done. It's impossible." Remember this, you can live a Christian life, never in your own strength, but with Christ living through your life.

A Part of My Journey

"Not in your own strength." After analyzing some of the things that have happened in my life, I have come to realize that I have tried to accomplish many things "in my own strength." Not that God didn't have his hand in those things, but he had to intervene many times to show me that there were certain things I was not supposed to do alone. He was gentle and patient with me, but I know I must have grieved him when I wouldn't allow myself to let him use his power within my life. You must understand this characteristic about me before I can tell you about an important part of my personal journey that I started with Jesus several years ago.

I cannot recall a time when I didn't love Jesus. I am sure it was because of the daily influence of my Christian parents. They placed me in situations at home, at church, and with friends where I couldn't keep from reading, seeing, and learning the way Christianity worked. Everything I heard about Jesus was that he was kind and gentle. This impressed me and was important to me because hatred and violence in any form have never been things I could understand.

I told my parents one evening that I wanted to become a Christian, to accept the promises I had learned about and to be a part of Jesus' love. As we started for church, I remember standing by the car and hearing my mother ask, "Are you sure you want to become a Christian?" As a nine-year-old girl, there was no doubt in my mind. After I made my final decision that night, the older Christians came by, shook my hand, and hugged me. I was sharing something with them that meant more than anything would ever mean again.

The next day I was walking down the road by myself, and as my thoughts rambled I thought about a girl I couldn't stand to be around. Actually, I was jealous of her. Then a fresh thought interrupted my thinking. *You shouldn't think like that. You're a Christian now.* I didn't know what to do with this new guilt I felt. I had not been told to confess my sins daily, after I became a Christian. I had already confessed before the church that I had accepted Christ as my Savior, the one who would save me from all my sins. What else was there to confess? It would be years before I would understand that I was to confess daily everything to God that displeased him and he would cleanse me each time. That was only one of the many things I didn't understand about being a Christian at the beginning.

Church activities became important to me. I did the normal amount of whispering, squirming, giggling, sleeping, and passing notes during the church services. All I remember about the pastor was that he preached loudly and would pound his fist on the pulpit. I had good, faithful Bible teachers. I still have in my possession a Bible storybook that I received from one of my teachers for attending Sunday School regularly. Something kept urging me and interesting me in being with other Christians. (I call it *something* because I was completely ignorant that Jesus had placed in each Christian's life the Holy Spirit to convict and guide.)

The pastor during my teen years was a graduate of a Christian college, and under his influence I chose to go there for my college education. I was continually surrounded at college by beautiful Christian people. I was grateful that I could be a part of such a fine Christian atmosphere. I listened to many sermons, for all the students were required to attend chapel services four times a week. Some of the sermons I heard caused me to doubt my personal meeting with God and others made me feel I wasn't doing nearly enough with my life.

Within two years I met and married a young man who was studying for the ministry, but I had no idea how his calling would affect my life. I began doing all the good things I felt were to be a part of my work as a pastor's wife. I sang in the choir. I attended all the book studies. I helped in Vacation Bible School. I led a youth group. I attended each night of every revival meeting. I participated in weekly visitation. These activities became so much a regular part of each day that it did not occur to me that I was doing entirely too much.

Later, my husband accepted an administrative position at a Christian college. We had three daughters by then and we were happy in our new location. I didn't waste any time getting involved in regular church activities again and at the same time I was trying to give my family equal time. I still didn't stop long enough to ask God what he wanted me to do.

Each time we moved, I found myself totally involved in numerous organizations. Even today, I have a question that flashes through my mind at times: *Was I doing what God was asking me to do all those years? Or was I doing those things because people were asking and I was accepting the jobs so people would think I was a good Christian?* That last thought has been extremely hard for me to face. I am sure God used some of these things I did for his glory. But it would have been more beneficial to my spiritual growth if, before starting anything, I had asked him if I was supposed to be doing all those things. I think about his generous love he extended to me during those early years as a young Christian, and I realize, more than I could have ever realized then, that he was extremely patient with me. He knew I wasn't quite ready to make a breakthrough into realizing that I would not always be able to do all these things in my own strength.

Later, I would be able to look back and see that I had not given much thought or thanks to how God kept me from injury, healed me when I was sick, led me to a Christian husband, allowed me to be the mother of three girls, gave me loving parents and friends, saw that I was never hungry, and always gave me shelter, laughter, and an inquisitive, sound mind.

A sound mind? Joking outwardly, but fearing inwardly at times when the girls were small and my husband was gone so much of the time, I would say, "I think I'm losing my mind." I had never thought to pray and ask God that he would give me a sound mind. I experienced some tormented years when I had guilt feelings mount up that I couldn't handle. I had unexpressed anger, I felt lonely, but I wanted to help keep my family happy so I completely smothered any negative feelings I had. I felt that my husband, because of his calling as a minister, had great faith, a strong hold on prayer, and life all figured out. How I wanted that for myself! How could he be so sure of his faith? I didn't feel I could talk with him then about these feelings, but I did desire to have that kind of faith.

A few years ago several events began to happen that were to change the course of my life. I had been a Christian twenty-seven years before God turned me around and told me, in ways I never dreamed he would, to give up trying to please my husband, my daughters, other people, or myself. He wanted me to stop living in my own strength. He wanted my life; he would take care of everything else. He let me know that I was my problem. I kept getting in his way.

One morning I found myself lying in a hospital bed. It was quiet. I opened my eyes and I found myself saying softly, "The Lord is my Shepherd." I was in the hospital from complete physical and mental exhaustion. I was thirty-seven years old and worn out from trying to live my own life, at my own pace, and in my own strength.

I had a week to myself to think. I took long walks. I listened to quiet music. Friends sent me books to read. One friend sent me a new paraphrased edition of the Bible, and I couldn't lay it down. I hungered to know what was in it for me. I prayed, not just once a day, but many times throughout the day. I observed other people, some of whom had been hurting just like me. I took the time to look into their faces, and as they talked to me I began to love them.

When I went home, I had one doubt but it never did equal my determination to start to be the woman God wanted me to be. My husband not only accepted my decision, he welcomed it. He rejoiced with me in it—that's all I needed.

Please don't expect me to say now, "Since that time everything has been wonderful." It hasn't. I am still imperfect. I continue to have many thoughts I should never allow to be conceived in my mind. I have said things that I would like to retract. I have misused time, and I have abused my body physically. At times I have been afraid for my own life, doubting God's daily protective care for me. I have doubted God's power to use my life. I have not always been a grateful child to my heavenly Father. But instead of all these imperfections bogging me down and stunting my spiritual growth I can keep going back to the basic belief that I accepted when I started on my spiritual journey with God as a child. I know that God loves me even with my imperfections.

I would have preferred not to have gone through such a fearful time in my life in the hospital. I would have liked to experience an easier way to know God better. From this experience I have come to understand more about praying, confessing, praising God, living with God, recognizing his strengths and my weaknesses, accepting the sureness of his forgiveness and his love. All these things are such an integral part of my life now that I cannot possibly see it being lived any other way.

Your Journey

It is not for me to know or to understand where you are at this time in your journey with God. Maybe you are going through extremely difficult times. I want to encourage you to recreate in your mind the faith you accepted the day you became a Christian. That faith is that God loves you, in spite of any difficulties you may encounter, of any weakness you may have. He is the one who will always be your strength if you will allow him to be. Every day he will show you a little more of what he wants you to give him. He will reveal it little by little as you can take it, absorb it, and make it become the all-important factor in your life.

After Jesus had finished telling the parable of the mustard

21

seed, the Scriptures record, "He used many such illustrations to teach the people as much as they were ready to understand" (Mark 4:33). There is no way you can understand all that is involved in the Christian life at the beginning of your journey. God reveals it to you as you are able to understand it.

The on-the-surface feelings you had about God in the beginning will take on greater depths of understanding as the years go by. You will start to realize that God uses even your smallest amount of knowledge about him to help you grow. You will begin to rely on his forgiveness as you have never experienced from anyone else before. God will begin placing other people in your life, showing you what he has done and is doing in their lives, and, at the same time reassuring you he can do the same with your life. You will begin to understand that even unpleasant, unexpected circumstances will play an important part in your growing up. You will begin talking with him about everything that concerns you.

At the beginning of my Christian life, I didn't know that God would be interested in everything that pertained to my life. I came to understand that God does not consider anything too small to talk with him about. I slowly began to have faith that he would eventually take over my entire being and would be patient with me during that growing-up time. But, even believing this about God, I still cling to ideas, thoughts, and actions that I know are wrong and that I need to ask God about so he can help me with each situation. It took me years to understand that my sinful nature had declared war on my new spiritual nature from the first moment of my young Christian life. (This is such an important fact to be discovered and understood by all Christians that I have gone into detail about these two natures in chapter 3.) Even with this daily warfare, I stand firm in my belief that God still loves me. As long as I continue to experience his forgiving, patient love, I know my life will have value and meaning.

Someone has written, "At each stage of his life, Jesus was what God wanted him to be." This is a worthy goal for your life and mine, but do not become discouraged or too critical of yourself when you become impatient with your spiritual development.

A gardener plants a seed in the very best soil and location. He nurtures it with plant food, and gives it the right amount of water and sunlight. All of this care is essential for the plant to bloom and flourish. The day comes when he sees a tight bud forming on the end of the stem. The gardener will not force the bloom by pulling on the tender petals to help them open more quickly. That would only bruise the petals and the flower would never be quite as beautiful as if he had waited for it to bloom in its own time. Because he is patient, the bud becomes larger, swells, and when it can no longer be contained, its beauty bursts forth in full bloom.

There is nothing fast about the development of a Christian's life. There are those moments when things will occur in your life when you feel you have immediate knowledge of the ways of God. But most of the time you must be willing to be patient with God's gentle wisdom. Don't become frustrated when your days are not instant successes. Relinquish the hold you think you have on life and believe that God will do his own scheduling with the development of your life.

A plant depends on you to follow all the necessary directions in order for it to mature into a healthy plant. I can remember my first try at planting a small flower bed. The seeds were supposed to be planted where they would have access to the eastern sunlight. They were supposed to be planted shallowly and the ground was to be kept moist. I did plant them on the

23

eastern side of the house. I did plant them shallowly, but I planted them so close to the house they could not get any moisture. I didn't fertilize the soil and I failed to water the plants regularly. The end result was an almost barren flower bed with the exception of a few blooms that were too stubborn to give up.

That flower bed is an apt comparison to my Christian growth. So many times I have made attempts to help my faith to grow and in my rush of daily living I have not found the time to nourish my starving soul. I have had to learn to depend on God to show me how to live, how to grow, how to conquer my fears. Above all, I have to depend on God to help me understand that to be the person God wants me to be, I cannot compare my life with other peoples' lives.

The experiences you and I have in our Christian journey will be different from anyone else's. Don't waste your time comparing your life with someone else's. God doesn't want you to strive for goals that are meant for others to accomplish. You are not going to have to live up to the American success story. Your primary satisfaction will be to live your own life the way you feel God wants you to live it. All that you are capable of becoming, every life that touches your life, every thought you have, every ambition you pursue will help you develop into the complete person God wants you to be.

You will want to work at being your real self. You will want to hold out your hand to God, feel his firm grasp, and know with assurance that your venture into faith is beginning. Your faith activates when you take your first step toward the unknown in your life. You will trust God to help you as you begin.

Did you ever play *Trust*? The rules were for you to stand with your back toward another person, close your eyes, and fall back, trusting the person behind you to catch you. There was always the pessimist who would have to look out of the corner of his eye to make sure the other person had his arms out, ready to catch him. The optimist took his turn, and, in full trust, without looking back, immediately fell into the arms of the one who was to catch him. Trust is depending on God, not looking back, not questioning your abilities, but in full trust allow God to help you be whatever he wants you to be. "You can never please God without faith, without depending on him" (Heb. 11:6a).

How do you learn to trust him more with your life? If you have this desire to develop a deeper level of trust with God, tell him. Tell him you want to please him with your life. Daily ask him to give you the faith you will need to do this.

Sharon's Journey

I want to share a story with you about a woman who has found it necessary to trust God more and more with her life. Hers was a slow beginning, but today she can tell you that God's way with her has developed her Christian life in a way she never thought would be possible. The process of trusting has not been easy, but she continues to show that she is becoming the person God expects her to be. Perhaps you will see reflected in her story the type of trusting person you could strive to become.

Sharon was fourteen years old when she personally met Jesus as her Savior. She regularly attended church the next three years, feeling she was maturing to some extent in her new Christian life.

When she was seventeen years old, she met and married a young man who was not a Christian. After their marriage, Sharon stopped attending church. It didn't bother her much

25

until two children were born into their home. As the girls began to grow, Sharon felt they should be in church, but her husband saw no need of this.

After ten years of marriage, many problems erupted between Sharon and her husband. When her life was physically threatened by him, she made the decision to end her marriage. This was a difficult decision because Sharon did not believe in divorce, but she felt she had no other choice than to dissolve their marriage.

She had to assume all the financial responsibilities for herself and the children. Shortly after the divorce was finalized, Sharon rented an apartment and began working in a factory to meet her financial obligations. She began taking sedatives in order to sleep at night and more pills to relieve severe headaches. The medicine for her headaches helped her through the day, and the sedatives helped her sleep at night.

Several months later she met a man at the factory where she worked and started dating him. After several evenings with him, she found he drank heavily and she began drinking with him. After one such night, Sharon came home, took her medicine, and went to bed. Early that morning she woke up extremely sick. Her first thought was, *I'm going to die and there will be no one to take care of my girls.* Overcome with fright, she prayed, "God, please help me straighten out my life."

She stopped dating the man she had met shortly after her divorce. A month later she met a Christian man at work. They began dating. One evening he asked her why she didn't go to church. She replied, "Because I don't have a car." He began going by for her and the children every Sunday. After several weeks of attending church, Sharon's oldest daughter accepted Jesus as her personal Savior.

Sharon eventually married this man. She and her daughter asked for membership in the church, feeling it was important that they worship as a family.

But even during this time when she felt her life was getting straightened out, Sharon continued taking sedatives. She had decreased her dosage but she remained dependent on them. One day she threw all the bottles away. She had some difficult days afterwards, but with God's help she overcame the habit.

Shortly after this Sharon's youngest daughter became sick with a serious blood disease that had been caused by a rare virus. Sharon prayed, "Lord, I give my daughter to you. Just give me strength to face whatever happens." After praying she felt better. She couldn't say she knew her daughter would get well; she only knew she had received the strength for which she had asked.

Sharon continued to pray. Eight days later her daughter left the hospital. In two months she was completely healed. She and her husband were so grateful to the Lord for what he had done that they couldn't do enough to show their gratitude. They took responsibilities in practically every organization of the church. Everything they were doing was good, but they became exhausted.

During one special church service Sharon and her husband sat in the audience listening to some Christians sharing what God was doing in their lives. These people were to show Sharon and her husband that what they needed in their lives was the assurance of peace and genuine joy that only God could give them and that they could not find it by "being busy."

That night the young couple knelt and prayed together for the first time. They asked God to take control of their lives. They told him that they desired to have a daily walk with him.

Giving God What You Are

Sharon says, "I thank God for his love and his forgiveness and for cleansing me from my sins so that I can become new before Jesus each day. I am not perfect, I have only begun to be what God wants me to be. I'm just a Christian under construction, as Jesus the carpenter changes my life. I love him and praise him for all his wondrous works."

You, like Sharon, will also have choices to make with your life. You have personally met Jesus, now allow him to work through you and take possession of your life. Be convinced that God can use you where you are by giving your entire self to him. Learn everything you possibly can about him. Accept every opportunity he gives you, great or small. He will take your willingness to learn and make something beautiful from it.

2
Getting Acquainted with God

There is no way to contain the understanding of God in the pages of a book when his very name means eternity. When you feel you have learned all you possibly can, you discover something else about God which only enhances your love for him. You will find out that he always acknowledges your desires as you "hunger and thirst after righteousness" (Matt. 5:6, KJV). He will acknowledge your request when you ask him to help you see the goodness in other people as he has seen it in you. You will want other people to experience this "peace of God, which passeth all understanding" (Phil. 4:7, KJV), as you are experiencing it.

God can do everything through you. He loves you and he wants you to be able to relate your entire life to him. People have tried various ways to relate their lives to God and to get better acquainted with him.

Musicians have composed lyrics to create expressions of their deepest love for God. Scientists have tried to discover all the wonders of the beginnings of creation in order to explain the power of God. Philosophers have delved into an inexhaustible study to understand the wisdom of God. Poets have searched for appropriate words to interpret the matchless beauty of God. Bible scholars have given years of study to help other people understand the riches and eternal promises of God's very own words.

Giving God What You Are

And you — you will get to know God more personally in your own way. You may have come from a home where your parents loved God supremely. They may have given you your first introduction to God. Therefore, you have had a basic beginning in your knowledge of God. However, you may be a person who grew up in a home having only heard God's name taken in vain. Your parents and friends might have seen no value in experiencing God in their daily lives, and, yet, you have personally felt this need. You do not fully understand why you have had this personal encounter with God, but in faith you have come. You are now one of God's children, and you want to learn all about him and the new life he has opened up to you. You want to know what he expects from you. He will never demand anything that is beyond your strength and ability. However, you may be too critical of yourself. You may become impatient because you won't feel that you are progressing rapidly enough in your spiritual development.

You will want to find your own way of becoming totally saturated in living with God — talking to him, pleasing him, loving him, and honoring him with your life. This complete merging with God will help you understand that God is with you in all of your life's circumstances. God knows that you cannot understand all there is to know about him at the start of your Christian life, but he will begin to give you every opportunity to know what he can do with your life. The giving of your life to him is your starting point. A more complete response will come as you begin "learning to know God better and better" (Col. 1:10b).

You can be guaranteed that the more you learn, the more you will stand in wonder of the fact that God, this one who cannot be compared and who has no limits, has become the most important being in your life. You stand in wonder that in all his majesty and authority, God has accepted you as one of his children.

Remain firm in the belief that your life is eternal, that you will continue your existence after your physical death, and that you have chosen to have that eternal existence with God. How significant God becomes in your life will be determined by your willingness and openness to learn about him.

Promise God now that you are willing to spend the remaining part of your life learning about him, listening to him, and believing in him so you won't limit his power in your new life. New insights about God will be coming to you constantly. With a daily fresh inflowing of thoughts about God, you will have the beginnings of God making you into a new person.

Most people start their Christian life by understanding very little about God except that they have recognized him as the one who sent his Son to save them from their sins. They accept that belief and when they act upon it, they become God's children. The anticipation of growth as a Christian is now at its starting point. You will discover that within the meaning of eternity lie all the characteristics that anyone would ever hope to find in the one true God.

There is no other god on this earth that can claim this truth: "In the beginning God" (Gen. 1:1, KJV). The first words in the Bible begin with this powerful affirmation. Look at the word *beginning.* It is defined as the first origin, the first source, to originate, to come into existence. There is absolutely no other god that originated in this way. All other gods are man-made. God is self-existent. "Before anything else existed, there was Christ, with God. He has always been alive and is himself God. He created everything there is—nothing exists that he didn't make" (John 1:1-3).

This knowledge of God might be somewhat difficult to

comprehend, because of the fact that in your lifetime you have always been able to trace everything you have learned or heard about to some beginning because of the work of another person. No one can take credit for any existing thing. The things people have created have been created because God gave them the materials and the minds to accomplish these things. All things exist because of the one who first existed. Where did he come from? Very simple. He has always been.

God, the Creator

God spoke the world into existence, and in the final act of power over all living things he created a man and a woman in his own image. Because God made you and me in his image, we are the only distinctive part of his creation that is privileged to come into his presence and receive an audience with the King himself.

God did not leave anything out of his creation. He knew what the beauty of the heavens could do to renew the soul of a person. He knew the pleasure that would come from blossoming flowers. He knew the necessity of water, air, and food. He knew how we would enjoy trees that produce food and shade. He knew the importance of darkness and light, the delight that the seasons would bring, the eternal hope that is felt in springtime.

God could have made some cutbacks. He could have left out the flowers, shade trees, grass, snow, or birds. But it pleased God to give us beauty and brilliant colors. He wanted his world to be a lovely place. To complete his world, so others could enjoy it with him, God created people. The most complex system ever to be made went into the creation of the human body.

God wants you to perfect your life, a life that you may have felt was worthless before you discovered the Supreme Power and allowed that power to begin to live in you. Now God is your personal God. He tells you that you will not only live, but that you will live more abundantly. God, who could foresee all things, could look at his finished creation and say without any hesitation, "It was very good" (Gen. 1:31, KJV).

As you begin to understand more of the nature of eternity and your being a part of it, there will be released within you a reverence for God and a faithfulness to the only one who can give you hope while living upon this earth and the promise of an eternal existence with him. He will continually remind you that he is the God who can bless your life. He has given you everything, even your "breath" (Gen. 2:7, KJV).

You are going to be excited about living as you begin to possess God's power, a power that can do anything. His creative powers within a person's life are unequaled. Not only does he have the power to create, he has the power to maintain what he has created, and that includes you.

God Is Everywhere

God's power is evident throughout the world, and, as hard as it might be to explain, his power is in no way limited by geographical boundaries. Simply stated, God is everywhere. Because God does not have a physical body, he cannot be limited by time or space. You are going to experience times when you feel that you are away from God, completely out of his presence. You will feel you are living out your life alone. But God will always be present. "I can never get away from my God" (Ps. 139:7b).

Discipline your mind to develop a keen awareness that God continually lives within your life and will always let his presence be known and felt. There are no words eloquent enough

33

to give a perfect conception of the immensity of his presence; he is in every person's life throughout the world.

God is with people facing problems and decisions. He is with those who are ill or facing death. He is with quiet people and rebellious people. He is with the greatest political figures and with those who have no social position. He is with knowledge-able people and with those who are uneducated. He is with the criminal and the saint. Whatever the category, God is with all people, at all times, under all circumstances. God loves you too much to ever let you stand alone in any situation.

A young mother told about trying to explain to her daughter, Laura, the fact that God is everywhere. After she had talked with her daughter, Laura didn't make any com-ment. The next day she and her mother went shopping. As they were driving to town, Laura began waving and continued to do so for quite some time. Her mother noticed but re-mained silent. Soon Laura smiled and winked at her mother, saying, "We know who I'm waving at, don't we, Mom!"

By becoming conscious of God's presence, you will begin feeling and seeing evidences of his presence and his generous expressions of love. Everything your eyes see, your ears hear, your hands touch, will be evidences of God. You will have summits of inspiration when you feel extremely close to God. Other times you will be in low places of discouragement and feel alone. But most of your Christian life will be spent on the plains of daily living, moving slowly forward with God. Wherever you feel as you are right now—satisfied, happy, successful, or defeated, disillusioned, frustrated—all you need to do is to renew your trust in God and know without a doubt that his firm grasp surrounds your life.

Consider the story of the prophet Elijah. He realized how sinful his nation was becoming. He worshiped God, but the majority of the people worshiped Baal, a worship which included sexual perversions and the sacrifice of babies. Jezebel, wife of King Ahab, was the person responsible for leading the people into Baal worship.

Elijah prayed. "Lord, show these people how wrong it is not to worship God. Don't let it rain for three years, just to show them who God really is." God heard Elijah's prayer. It didn't rain for three years. After three years Elijah met with Ahab and challenged Ahab to meet him on a certain mountain. Ahab was to bring all the prophets of Baal with him so they could compete with Elijah in a praying contest. The winner of the contest would prove who served the only true God.

They brought two bulls to be sacrificed. The prophets of Baal prepared their sacrifice and laid it upon the altar of wood. They didn't put a fire under the sacrifice because they were to pray that their god would send fire to burn up the sacrifice.

The prophets of Baal began. They called upon their god from morning until noon, but there was no answer from Baal. They prayed louder but still nothing happened.

After noon had passed, it was Elijah's turn to call upon his God. Elijah took twelve stones and built an altar. He dug a ditch around the altar. He then placed wood on the altar and laid the sacrifice on the wood. He asked some of the prophets of Baal to fill four barrels with water and pour it on the sacrifice and the wood. He asked them to do this three times until the ditch was filled with water, also. Then Elijah prayed:

O Lord God of Abraham, Isaac, and Israel, prove today that you are the God of Israel. Then suddenly, fire flashed down from heaven and burned up the young bull, the wood, the stones, the dust, and even evaporated all the water in the ditch! (1 Kings 18:36, 38).

Elijah not only prayed to God to withhold the rain but he

also prayed that God would send fire from heaven and burn up the sacrifice. Elijah was elated after God answered his prayer. Before the day was over, however, God would see Elijah, virtually in the depths of despair running for the darkness of a cave.

Elijah had a legitimate reason for his despondency. Jezebel had confronted him in a fit of rage. "Elijah, you just wait and see. Tomorrow you are going to be dead. I will personally see that you are!"

Elijah began running to get away from Jezebel's threats. He began to pray, but this time it was a totally different kind of prayer. "Lord, I've had all I can take. Just let me die." But in Elijah's time of despair, God was with him. God understood this area of Elijah's life, also. He didn't leave him alone when he was tired or afraid.

Because of his exhaustion, Elijah felt self-pity. He thought he was the only person alive who was earnestly serving God. Since he felt everyone had deserted him, he felt that he might as well give up, too. Elijah found a cave in which to hide. He began asking God to do something spectacular as he had done on the mountain, but God had to let Elijah know that he does not always act in this way in order to allow his presence to be felt.

In one day Elijah had reached out and grasped the power and presence of God. In the same day he experienced a frightening, lonely time of despair, and yet God was not through with this man. God wanted him to get up and get started back on his journey.

Elijah did not have many more experiences as he had had on the mountain with the prophets of Baal, but instead he walked along slowly, moving toward what God was asking him to do. There could be no doubt that God would always be with him.

God Has All-Knowledge

God knows every need you will ever have. He knows about the daily battles you are having in your life. He knows the desires you have for accomplishing good with your life, the secrets that you don't want other people to know, the hurts you try so hard to hide.

God knows everything that is possible to know about you. He has all knowledge of all things. Without searching to find answers, he knows about the workings of the laws of nature. He has set everything into motion. His knowledge is immediate. He knows when each sparrow falls, "and he knows the number of hairs on your head!" (Luke 12:7a). "He counts the stars and calls them all by name" (Ps. 147:4).

Since God knows all, you do not have to go before God and try to explain anything. If you have done something that you know has displeased God, he knows about it before you tell him. It becomes a cleansing process when you ask him to forgive you and to pick you up and help you start again.

Did you ever try to hide the evidence when you disobeyed your parents? I can remember as a child that my parents thought milk of magnesia or castor oil would cure any illness. One day my mother handed me my dose of medicine and left the room. After she closed the door, I noticed a healthy house plant sitting on a small table. I felt the plant needed the medicine worse than I did. I poured the medicine into the soil. My mother never found out about that act of disobedience, but God not only knew about it, he saw me perform it.

You can think of times when you have deceived others and yourself, but God has known and seen you in your deception every time. He has all knowledge of all things. You have been successful at reaching certain goals in your life. God has watched you in your endeavors, seen you accomplish, and

37

experienced your satisfaction with you. But how good it is for him to hear you thank him for giving you the ability and the drive to succeed. God has given you many happy, eventful days. Sometimes you feel it is impossible to thank him adequately, but be assured he knows those unspoken joys. He was already sharing those happy times with you, and in that quiet sharing time you became aware of God.

You have continuous opportunities to relate all the experiences of your life to God. Every time you share an event with God, good or bad, you are making it possible for him to relate to you. In order for you to learn more quickly about this personal relationship you have with God, never stop reading God's Word, never stop learning about his vast knowledge, never stop looking to him for answers, never stop believing his truth. In this learning process, you will learn to know what God's kind of love is all about.

God's Love

God surely foresaw the difficulty you would have at being able to explain his kind of love to other people, so he helped you out. He wrote about that love, but even after you read God's own words, it can still be difficult to believe such an unselfish, complete love. It is only after seeing that love, feeling it, experiencing its warmth and eternal security, and accepting it, that you are able to know the beginnings of such a wondrous love.

And I pray that Christ will be more and more at home in your hearts, living within you as you trust him. May your roots go down deep into the soil of God's marvelous love, and may you be able to feel and understand, as all God's children should, how long, how wide, how deep, and how high his love really is, and to experience this love for yourselves, though it is so great that you will never see the end of it or fully know or understand it (Eph. 3:17-19a).

Getting Acquainted with God

There are times when I pause in my quiet moments and try to visualize how this gift of love was purchased. I can see myself standing at the cross with others. As I stand there looking up into Jesus' face, I feel that perfect love searing my heart. It is almost as if he were looking down at me and saying, "I am doing this for you." I will never believe that this is only a story about a good man. I will not believe that the story about this man ended here. I do believe that this great one came to this earth, a spiritual God taking on a human form, and became one of us. It was so you and I could finally understand what he had been saying all along. "I love you. I love you with the kind of love you have never known until you began to believe in the kind of love I have to offer. There will be those who will refuse to understand my love, but that won't discourage me. I will keep defying rejection, and I will keep offering my love to anyone who will accept it.

"My love offers communion with God himself, although I know there will be those who, through their belief in their self-importance and self-sufficiency, will choose to worship *their* successes, *their* intellect, *their* talents, and *their* earthly possessions."

After this encounter at the cross, I find I can no longer bear to look into the anguished face of Jesus. I no longer feel worthy to be looking at him. Nothing seems appropriate to say, but in my faltering way I know he'll understand. "God, thank you for sending your kind of love into my world so I can see it, claim it for my very own. Help me to be capable of responding to your kind of love. Amen."

I leave this mental scene, and in that sacred quiet time with God, I know he gave me everything he had. It all went into his love. He lived out his love, and finally he died for it. That kind of love has come to mean the only sure way of life.

Giving God What You Are

There can be no doubt in your mind that God, who created everything, also created love. Within this meaning of God's love is another word that is a further extension of his love and that word is *grace*. You will hear songs about God's grace, you will hear people sharing personal experiences of God's grace, and when you have personally grasped its meaning you will be unable to remain silent when you have the opportunity to share the meaning of God's grace with someone else.

An older Christian woman caused an event to occur in my life that pulled together everything God had ever been trying to show me all along—that his love completely surrounds me and it will eventually capture my entire being. This knowledge came about when I finally understood the meaning of God's grace.

I had known Jerry for two years. She and I worked in the same office building. We became acquainted by talking with each other at office breaks or when we passed each other outside our offices. Later I gave up my secretarial job so I would be able to devote more time to writing.

A few months later I was invited back to visit with the other secretaries and friends. Each one caught me up on what was happening in their lives. Inevitably, someone asked me how my writing was coming along. I told them I had received numerous rejection notices, but I wasn't discouraged. Half jokingly, I said I might have to start my writing career by organizing a cookbook. But I went on to say that a friend of mine had just done that and it had cost her $300 to have her cookbook published. In addition she had to do her own publicizing and selling. First of all, I didn't have $300, and I also had not planned to do my own selling. The conversation changed to my family and what they were doing. Jerry excused herself, but before she left she asked me to stop by her office.

Getting Acquainted with God

Before I left the building I stopped to see her. We talked awhile and then she handed me an envelope. It was two days before Thanksgiving and since Jerry was known in the office for giving cards for all occasions, I felt this card was in keeping with her thoughtfulness. On front of the envelope she had written, "Do not open until Thanksgiving." After we finished our visit, I started home. I laid the envelope on the seat next to me. As I drove home, I came to an unusually long stop light. It gave me time to glance at the envelope and that's all I needed. I picked it up and immediately opened it.

The note read: "With love, Jerry. No strings attached." In back of the note was a check for $300. I began crying. I didn't deserve that check. I knew Jerry had given it to me to help me fulfill my desire to write. It had been given to me as a gift of encouragement. And although I had not yet accomplished anything with my writing at that time, Jerry believed in me.

This is my understanding of God's grace. It is the total activity of God in the whole human experience. He hands you and me his gift of grace, with no strings attached. How could he, this God who is so powerful, so matchless, so unchanging, love persons like you and me enough to make such a sacrifice in order to make the gift of grace available to everyone? He does, because he continually shows us day after day that with his kind of love there are no strings attached. Grace—something so priceless you cannot buy it for any price, but God has given it away.

After I received and accepted the gift from my friend, I tried to decide what I could possibly do to show my gratitude and to make Jerry understand how that gift would have a continued effect on my life from that day on. I went to the florist and chose a beautiful crystal bud vase. I looked at the flowers and found a delicate pink rosebud to place into the vase. Still

41

undetermined as to what I would write on the card, I asked God to help me write the words of thankfulness. I had the flower delivered and, upon its delivery, I trusted God to speak to that precious friend through that lovely flower and the message I felt he had helped me write.

I still feel unworthy of that gift each time I think back to that lovely winter day when God showed me, through another person, the impact of the knowledge of his grace.

Like Jerry's gift, I cannot think of any gift that could excel God's generous gift of love. Therefore, I cannot help believing that God would have me respond to his love by offering more of my life to him and by desiring to maintain the life with which he would be pleased. There will always be a feeling of unworthiness, but I know I can come before him with the very best I have to offer and he will accept it in the love with which it has been given.

In God's limitless creativity, he reveals the supreme example of his love. One of his many ways has been shown by his adopting people as his children. Once this adoption has taken place it will never under any circumstances be broken. "His unchanging plan has always been to adopt us into his own family by sending Jesus Christ to die for us. And he did this because he wanted to!" (Eph. 1:5). In biblical times a slave could be adopted by the family that owned him. When this decision was made by the slave owner, he would pay a price for the slave in front of witnesses. The slave was then considered born again into a new family. He then had the same privileges as the other children and even became an heir to the father's possessions.

Jesus paid the price for you in order for you to become one of God's children. No one will ever be able to break that union. You have the same privileges as all of his children. You cannot imagine all that you have inherited until the day comes when the total value is revealed to you by God himself.

You will be confronted by people who will try to shake your beliefs or who will try to make you compromise, but no one will ever be able to destroy the personal experience of your knowing that you belong to God, forever. A young Christian was trying to explain to a group how he felt about the permanency of his personal relationship with God. He held out his hands. He opened one hand and said: "Pretend you are standing in the middle of my hand. This hand represents the world in which you are living. Now I close my hand around you. This represents Jesus surrounding your life. Now I put my other hand completely around my closed hand. This represents God." He smiled and concluded: "I dare anyone to try to go through God and then through Jesus to get to me and then try to persuade me that I will not always be one of God's children. I will always belong to God. This is my everlasting security as his child. This is my spiritual inheritance."

God . . .

So complex, yet simple to receive.

So vast, yet so personal.

So limitless, yet always close by.

So powerful, yet gentle.

So knowledgeable, yet understanding.

So perfect, yet forgiving.

This God,

I am his,

And he loves me.

3
Realizing How Much God Loves You

When I look up into the night skies and see the work of your fingers—the moon and the stars you have made—I cannot understand how you can bother with mere puny man, to pay any attention to him! And yet you have made him only a little lower than the angels, and placed a crown of glory and honor upon his head (Ps. 8:3-5).

If you skipped reading the above verses, go back and read them carefully. They're about you. God is revealing to you that in the vastness of the world he has created, you are the one whom he loves supremely. It is inconceivable how God could love the persons he created so much that he would place upon his Son the sins of the entire world.

As you enter into the transition period of a new spiritual life, you will become more aware than ever of how important it is for you to accept yourself the way God accepts you. Sit quietly for a moment. Look at everything around you. Look out at the sky, the clouds, the stars, the trees. Listen to all the sounds you can hear and say with the psalmist, "I cannot understand how you can bother with mere puny man" (Ps. 8:4a).

All along, God has had a distinct purpose for you. You will not fully understand at first everything that is going to be yours as his child. But eventually, as you learn to hold nothing back from God, you will be able to go beyond what you have been and develop the potential of what you are capable of becoming through him. Jesus has said, "Whosoever believeth in him should not perish, but have everlasting life" (John 3:16b, KJV). "Whosoever" includes all ages, races, sizes, and temperaments. It includes the bold, the timid, the rich, the poor. No person needs to be left out. This is the immensity of the power and love God manifests to make all lives useful, meaningful, and hopeful.

When you begin to understand God's love for you, you will want to cultivate and develop the spiritual person within you. This growth will lead you to lasting experiences in which God allows you to marvel at the power he can perform in your life through him. It will cause your spiritual self to succeed. You are not to emulate someone you consider to be the ideal person. God begins using you just the way you are right now. "But by the grace of God I am what I am: and his grace which was bestowed upon me was not in vain" (1 Cor. 15:10a, KJV).

Say this verse over and over, memorize it, write it where you can see it each day. God accepts you the way you are today. As you grow through him, he will accept those areas of growth as well. You are asked to present your body to God as a living sacrifice. Dedicate your whole personality to God. Are there some areas of your life that you have not given to God — your vocation, your finances, your leisuretime, your possessions? As you mature in your faith, you will become aware of the areas that have not been turned over to God. Allow him to enter every facet of your life — everything that occupies your days.

God's Plan for You

You will develop your spiritual life continuously as you learn more about God's love for you. Your life will encompass not only your spiritual growth but your whole being, everything that affects and influences your life.

Before you became a Christian, and even afterwards, you

may have spent a large portion of your time trying to please other people. But you will delay your spiritual growth if you place greater importance on what people expect of you rather than what God expects of you. You will be amazed at how God can develop your life as you seek out his way for you. He tells you to "Call unto me, and I will answer thee, and shew thee great and mighty things, which thou knowest not" (Jer. 33:3, KJV).

You will want God's approval of your life. He knows your abilities as well as your limitations. He will never ask the impossible from you. When you find yourself using all your energy doing "good" things, stop awhile and ask yourself: "Does God want me to be this busy? What am I trying to prove? Why do I feel I must say 'yes' every time someone asks me to do something? Wouldn't I enjoy my life more if I would stop long enough to do some self-searching and ask God what he is wanting me to do?"

If you have trouble distinguishing between God's direction and man's demands, pray for the wisdom you need to handle your immediate situation. With God's help, you can eliminate this constant rushing through your life.

Your life will not be constructed in the same manner as the lives of other Christians. God looks at you as a special person. There is no one more important than you are as far as he is concerned. He sees your potential. You will never realize or be aware of it if you do not acknowledge it. Begin trying to understand your worth as he sees it in you.

As you begin to feel genuine love for yourself, you will nurture and encourage yourself, admit your failures, acknowledge your abilities, and pray for yourself. There is no egotism in these acts. These are natural results of recognizing your worth as an individual through God.

Realizing How Much God Loves You

Spend some time getting acquainted with yourself. With today's accelerated rate of living very few people see the significance of this. Discover why you do some of the things you do. It's a tremendous experience to get off to yourself, to think about yourself, your potentials, the things you desire to do in this life, and what you want to accomplish with the abilities God has given you.

You begin to become a confident person when you acquire more knowledge of yourself and your abilities. If you haven't done this until now, concentrate on the abilities you know you have. This isn't bragging; it's realizing what God has placed in your life in order for you to do certain things for him. He knows what you would like to be, but he accepts what you are, what you have been. He uses these beginnings to accomplish his purpose with you.

When you decide what your abilities are, you are ready to enter into some of the greatest opportunities of your life. You accepted Christ in faith. Now, in faith, believe that you have been created to be somebody. A guest speaker announced to a group of students that he would be speaking on the subject "Accepting Self." Before the lecture began there were many who had to be turned away. Every available chair and floor space had been filled. This gave evidence that Christians are continually seeking ways of being able to accept themselves. Why is this such a battle? Do you strive to reach goals that are not yours to attain? Are you trying to please or impress others? Are you trying to do what your friends are doing? Accepting what is right for you is another great secret to learn about your life.

Consider your potentials, even if you feel they are insignificant. An effective place to start would be to do today what you know you are capable of doing. This may be as simple as talking or listening to someone, writing a note to a special friend, giving another person some encouragement, being thoughtful to your family, talking to a lonely person on the telephone. These would not be considered unimportant to the persons receiving these gifts. You will grow as you use your talents, no matter how unimportant they may seem to you.

Would you like to accomplish some worthy goals with your life? Don't ask yourself if you can do it. If God has given you the ability to accomplish and you acknowledge the fact that you have the ability, do it! A popular lecturer, while discussing this idea about each person being able to openly admit that God has given him certain abilities said: "Thank-you, God. I've got it, it's yours, now help me use it."

Take some time to understand your feelings and respond to your deep convictions. God's plan for you is different than his plan for anyone else. It won't happen all at once, but there will come a day when you will believe, without a doubt, how valuable you are in God's sight. Your value will reach out and affect other lives, so try releasing yourself in order to touch more lives.

Pray: "Lord, I am your child. Today and all my tomorrows I will do the best I can. I will practice turning everything over to you, even if it seems small to me at the time. Show me your will for my life and I will do it. Amen."

Understanding Your New Nature

A similar, daily prayer to God is essential because you are now dealing with a dual nature that was not present until you became God's child. You will need God's direction as you confront this new nature, in order to fulfill your life as God plans for it to be fulfilled.

You received a new spiritual nature when you became a Christian, but you did not lose your old, selfish nature. You can expect the two of them to be constantly at war with each other. You must understand this fact or it could shatter your faith. Read the following verses carefully. You may have to turn to them often as you deal with the determined, persistent strength of your old nature.

> I don't understand myself at all, for I really want to do what is right, but I can't. . . . When I want to do good, I don't; and when I try not to do wrong, I do it anyway. It seems to be a fact of life that when I want to do what is right, I inevitably do what is wrong. I love to do God's will so far as my new nature is concerned, but there is something else deep within me, in my lower nature, that is at war with my mind and wins the fight and makes me a slave to the sin that is still within me. So you see how it is: my new life tells me to do right, but the old nature that is still inside me loves to sin. Oh, what a terrible predicament I'm in! Who will free me from my slavery to this deadly lower nature? Thank God! It has been done by Jesus Christ our Lord. He has set me free (Rom. 7:15,19,21-25).

You will continue to experience uncontrolled anger, unjustified thoughts, envy, jealousy, greed, destructive criticism. You will be negligent with important matters, ignore time that should be spent with God and for God, have unwholesome motives and goals, and be untruthful with yourself and others. All Christians must deal with this old nature. All Christians are learning how to cope with and find ways of solving those things that should not be allowed to be a part of the Christian life.

Admit openly to yourself and to God the warfare that is within you. Confess that you have it. It has been there from the beginning. Observe a newborn baby. Examine the flawless body, see the soft lines of his lips, touch the tiny ears. You can't help but question how anything so innocent, so perfect, so helpless, could ever grow into a responsible person that will have to cope with the same physical and spiritual natures that you are having to deal with now.

These two natures will always be battling and making you

feel guilt that you never felt before you became a Christian. But you don't need to be a servant to any sin. No sin can have dominion over you now. "He will show you how to escape temptation's power so that you can bear up patiently against it" (1 Cor. 10:13b).

Satan's greatest weapon is to convince you that you can't win over your old nature. He'll try to get you to believe that you have no worth and that there's no need to keep trying because there's no way you can lead a perfect life. If he can get you to give in to your old nature, then he becomes the victor.

It might be that you have had, or are having, the problem of dealing with inferior feelings—you have no worth. Practically everyone has a problem with these at some time. Satan knows about this human weakness. He pounces on it and works tirelessly to keep you feeling unsure about yourself. If you know this is a problem in your life, make yourself come face to face with each inferior feeling. Recognize these feelings as being deficits in your life and realize that they must be understood, conquered, and controlled. Be persistent in believing you can overcome all things that hinder you from becoming a victorious Christian.

Christ Lives Through You

Now that you understand about your two natures, you will become more capable of dealing with the kind of life God wants you to live. How can you know you are living the kind of life God wants you to live? How can you know you are fulfilling the purpose for which God made you? It cannot be done alone, you must allow Christ to live through you. "I have been crucified with Christ: and I myself no longer live, but Christ lives in me. And the real life I now have within this body is a result of my trusting in the Son of God, who loved me and gave himself for me" (Gal. 2:20).

Realizing How Much God Loves You

With your world revolving around God, your life has taken on new dimensions, including all the good you do and every life you help. In life, through him, you actually become more relaxed, more positive, more creative, and more willing to use your faith. You will have to defy Satan many times and know that he is not strong enough to take away this joy from your new life. God will help you resist the hold that Satan may temporarily have on you.

Acknowledge God as the one who is in control. I have a dachshund. I was determined, even when she was a pup, that she would learn to take walks on a leash. She didn't know what to expect when the collar and leash were put on her for the first time. We started walking and she pulled so hard on the leash that she had trouble breathing. Neither of us enjoyed that first walk. The next day we started the same way but about half way through the walk she wasn't pulling nearly as hard against the leash. The next day she walked at my pace during the entire time. It was much more enjoyable for both of us.

I have related this idea to part of my knowledge about myself and I have had to ask: "How many times do I try to get too far ahead of God? How many times do I pull against him?" I should know by now that my life is much more pleasant when I live at the Master's pace. I continue to try to put into practice the truth of God living through me. In my desire to do this, I tell him that I do want to walk with him and not always be ahead of him in the things he would want me to do.

I have never fully enjoyed taking trips on an airplane. My husband has tried to get me to think positively about the beauty of viewing the world from above, but I always get the thought just before I step onto the plane that I'd rather be taking the trip by car. I start praying that the mechanics have done their job well and that there is plenty of fuel in the tank.

Giving God What You Are

I pray that the weather will be smooth and that we will have the very best pilot. Then I feel the plane taxi down the runway, and in an instant we are airborne. Very slowly I lean back in my seat and try to relax. I watch the flight attendant's facial expression to make sure everything is all right. Now that I'm locked in the plane and we are soaring far above the earth, I realize that since I have no knowledge about flying, I must completely rely on the pilot to get me to my destination.

You know now that you have God in control of your life. He wants to help you enjoy life as he intends for it to be enjoyed. You cannot run ahead of God any more than you can fly a plane because you don't have the knowledge to do so. You cannot conceive of the complete plan God has for your life, but he is revealing it a little at a time, as you are able to understand it and relate it to your personal life.

Seeing God in this perspective makes you willing to live your life through Christ because "He has given you the whole world to use, life and even death are your servants. He has given you all of the present and all of the future" (1 Cor. 3:22b).

Give God Your Life

God asks you to give him the reins. He knows you are limited in certain areas, but he'll make you strong in others. We are basically selfish. The idea of giving something away that is "mine" goes against the old nature. So the thought of handing over to God our bodies, our accumulated wealth, our material possessions might be hard to do willingly.

Can you remember when you were a small child and you had to share toys with your brothers and sisters? Most of the time each of you wanted to play with the same toy at the same time. You would end up tugging and screaming, "Mine, mine!" Why do you think you reacted that way? You weren't taught to say "mine," you just said it.

Realizing How Much God Loves You

You understand that as a Christian, your life is no longer yours, it's God's. But by your actions you might be continuing to say, "It's mine." So, accepting the idea of "giving up to have more" doesn't sound logical until you start giving yourself away—to God and to other people. You will be confined within yourself until you begin to use the potential that has been stored up within you for so many years. You begin feeling differently toward people. You can see there is good in everyone, and you can start loving them and understanding them in a way that is different than you have ever felt. They have worth just like you. You begin listening to what they're saying, how they're searching the same way as you are. You begin making yourself available to those people so that they will feel free to express even deeper feelings to you. People are yearning to be heard, to know that someone is interested in what they're saying. All of this is included in giving yourself away when you make yourself available to others. God will take these stirrings within you and convert them into something tangible for his good.

Steadily you are finding out more things about yourself and other people, why you react the way you do toward certain situations, why people say the things they say. God accepts your willingness to give this part of your life that you have recently handed him—the life you have called "mine" until now.

When you hand your life over to God you begin to experience the kind of living that fills every fiber of your existence. Because this truth of "dying to self" is so vital to my own life, I want to share with you how giving certain areas of myself to God has changed my life.

When I was forty years old, I began experiencing some searching in my life that I had trouble explaining. I was wanting to give another part of my life to God, but I was not fully

53

aware of what he was wanting me to give him. All I could ask was, "What do you want, Lord?" I prayed, but there were no dramatic changes. Before long I noticed that my daily routine remained the same, with one exception. I still loved my husband and my children, but I was loving them through God. I kept going to church, but it was because I loved God and not because I was expected to go.

I began praying differently. I was taking everything to God in prayer, even the things I thought had been too small to pray about before. I began to understand that a daily quiet time with God would prepare me for each day. I no longer permitted myself to dwell on the future or what might or might not happen. God was only asking me to take care of today.

During this time I was working as a part-time secretary, but this wasn't what I wanted to do for the rest of my life. For a long time I had had a secret desire to write. For awhile I was embarrassed to mention this to anyone—even God. I knew it would take time to develop this idea, but my days were so filled with my job, trying to keep up with my housework, and fulfilling my role as a wife and mother that I didn't see how I could fit writing into my schedule. The desire to write became so demanding that I gave up my job.

I began setting aside each morning exclusively for writing, unless an unavoidable emergency arose. The Lord and I knew that I didn't have any formal writing education. I prayed and told God that if he wanted me to write personal letters and touch one life at a time, I was willing to do that, but I also felt strongly that I wanted to write a book. I didn't know how to organize a book, so God guided me. He began flooding my mind with ideas and kept thoughts and words flowing that actually left me bewildered at times. I just knew after I started writing that I wanted to live long enough to get every thought down on paper.

Realizing How Much God Loves You

I believe in my work because I know, without a doubt, I am in the place God wants me to be. I still have not learned how to handle my feelings of gratitude appropriately. When, in the midst of my writing, I imagine myself in the presence of God after death, and I know all that I have ever read of him, heard about him, written about him, and seen in his creation—all of this will be magnified a million times. To share these joys and truths and not stifle one insight about him, will be one of the purposes for which he has allowed me to live upon this earth.

God's Purpose for You

You may ask, "What about my purpose?" Your purpose will be different because your life's plan and goals are different. You are learning how much God loves you and you believe in that love. Now you will want to ask him to reveal to you how you are to live your life through him. It is possible that your daily routine won't change that much, but your faith will be more firm, your love more real. You'll have a higher tolerance rate; your patience will last longer and you will be more positive about all aspects of life.

Stop your busy life more often and contemplate the simple life. From the world's standards, you may be poor. In your Christian growth, you will be shown that outward living counts for little when you feel God's gifts so deeply within your life. You are in continual preparation for eternity with God. You may stop to consider the fact in your living with God that no matter how successful you become, whether you have reached the summit of life—socially, intellectually, politically, scientifically, or financially—you still will not have reached the most important decision of your life in realizing that God must be the Lord of your life and accepting him as that.

Be willing to settle for less—wealth, social standing, recognition, anything that is offered to you—in order to live simply, to have peace, and know without a doubt that you are doing what God expects from your life.

You must feel that you can do something and master it. Do you still feel you do not have the resources necessary for your life? Begin to understand that God gives you anything you are lacking. Discipline yourself and allow time for correction while you are improving your life. Believe that God can do all things in and through your life.

God has made you, and he has made you to live with him. You don't want to let one moment of your life escape from you by merely considering the abundant life you might have through Christ. Right now you are capable of being the best God wants you to be.

Many years ago I heard about Jesus' beautiful, perfect life. Then I began to read about his birth and I could see and almost visualize touching that soft, perfect, little body. I found that Jesus had left a perfect home to become a person like me. I read how he overcame temptations, the same kind I would have. I found out how gentle he was with little children. I saw how his perfect hands could touch imperfect bodies and make them well. Every time I learn something new about God's love, I begin to understand more of his love for me. I know that God's love is an unselfish love, a love that has no bounds. His life is the beautiful life, and I have learned what I must do because of it.

Maybe you aren't happy with your life as it is now. But every life has to have new starts along the way. Why not start enjoying living now!

4
Talking with God

Now I lay me down to sleep.
I pray thee, Lord, my soul to keep.
If I should die before I wake,
I pray thee, Lord, my soul to take.
God bless Momma, Daddy, and Sister, too. Amen.

This is the first prayer I can recall saying as a small child. Another recollection of prayer I have is from an age when I was feeling self-sufficient, although at the same time I was struggling with my own worth and my future as a young adult. I had not yet experienced the full effect of a genuine prayer life.

I had always heard that it was important to pray, but every day? In my mind I felt every other day would be often enough. So I set to work making my long mental list about all the good things I was doing, trying to remember all my faults and all the people for whom I should be praying. By the second night—*all people pray just before they go to sleep,* I thought—I had an awfully lot of praying to do. I had two problems. I forgot many of the things I was going to pray about, and even if I had remembered, I would fall asleep before I finished. Therefore, I had to devise another strategy. I would sit by my bed (kneeling hurt my knees) and hope that this would at least keep me awake. It didn't!

Giving God What You Are

Since my sister and I shared a bedroom, she had to tolerate me during that summer. Later as I looked back on that period of my life, I wondered how she stood me; but more still, I wondered how the Lord stood me.

One evening just a few years ago, I was deeply distressed about a family problem. I had prayed, and I felt I had sincerely prayed in a way that the problem would pass. It didn't. Finally the situation came to a climax. My temper got out of control and, as a mother generally does, I began to blame myself for what had happened.

I felt completely helpless. Out of desperation I went to bed, but I didn't fall asleep. I began to pray. I had never prayed that way before that night, but I knew this—I loved my family and I wanted us to be united again. As I lay there, I whispered: "God, what is it? What on this earth am I to do? I've prayed about this matter but I have felt no peace. I'm still making a mess out of things. Instead of making a situation better, I'm making it worse. Do you want my life? If I died would that make everything right? Have I been selfish? What is it God?"

After I presented all these questions to God, I found myself verbally giving God everything I possessed. I gave him the house; I gave him every piece of furniture in the house. I gave him my clothes, the cars, and every material possession I could think of giving. But I wasn't through giving. I knew I had to present to him, as unselfishly as I knew how, my husband and my children, and finally I gave myself to him. I felt alone, empty. There was nothing left. I fell asleep. I had wrestled with my soul and I had won.

The problem was not gone the next morning, but I felt better. Within a year, the problem subsided and our family was closer to each other than we had been before.

Talking with God

After that incident, God started showing me ever so tenderly that I must lose my life and my dearest possession—my family—to him, completely. There was to be no other way. He expected no less.

I have shared with you three very meaningful times in my life involving prayer. I can look back at these times now and realize that no one learns all there is to know about prayer in one session with God. In a slow, steady progression in the construction of a life, God reveals what a Christian can inherit through prayer as his child.

When you come into God's presence, you recognize your weaknesses, your ignorance of what you should pray about. In the consciousness of your utter helplessness to pray as you should, you look to the Holy Spirit and throw yourself completely upon God so he can direct your prayers.

Why Christians Pray

"Were I a preacher, I should above all things preach the practice of the presence of God . . . an habitual, silent and secret conversation of the soul with God." These words from a seventeenth-century writer remind us that God wants us to pray. "And ye shall seek me, and find me, when ye shall search me with all your heart" (Jer. 29:13, KJV). Prayer means to possess the freedom to pray anytime, anywhere, on any occasion, about anything.

How can you make prayer an active part of your life? Do you consider praying when you are having a bad day, when you are worried about your health? Perhaps you are rushing, people may be pressuring you, maybe there just aren't enough hours in the day to get all your work done. Do you pray then? Would you like to stop awhile and rest and forget all the problems facing you in this chaotic world? Do you feel all these things

59

are unimportant to God? He says, "In every thing by prayer
. . . let your requests be made known unto God" (Phil. 4:6,
KJV).

Prayer is the means by which all your desires and your entire
life can be redirected into channels for God's will. It will help
you straighten out your priorities. Prayer is only for those who
want an abundant, adventurous life. It is difficult to know
what might happen if you got up each morning and prayed:
"God, today is yours. What do you want me to do with it?"
You will become spiritually strong, and be filled with God's
fullness. "But they that wait upon the Lord shall renew their
strength" (Isa. 40:31a).

In all humility you can't help but wonder how this one, so
great, will allow you to come into his presence. The beauty of
this is that no one has a monopoly on prayer. The person who
has lived the most wicked life can come to the place when he
can offer thanksgiving to God for giving his life purpose and
hope. The person whose life has been most exemplary can
offer acceptable thanks only in the same way. There is only
one way to approach God. "No man cometh unto the Father,
but by me" (John 14:6, KJV).

If you have not taken advantage of praying, then you have
not stopped long enough in your journey to fully comprehend
how it could affect your life. Abraham Lincoln said: "I have
been driven many times to my knees by the overwhelming con-
viction that I had nowhere else to go. My own wisdom and that
of all about me, seemed insufficient for the day." What could
happen to cause you to literally fall on your knees and lay
yourself completely stripped before God? It is because you
have nowhere else to go. Some of the problems or decisions you
face become so complex, your soul has no other alternative.
You cry for help, a help that when it comes is greater than any

human strength you could ever experience. That is why people pray. You can make praying as vital to your life as breathing. The fact that the Savior felt a need to pray magnifies the great need for prayer to be a daily, active ingredient in your life.

You must acknowledge the fact that prayer will change your life. Christians have learned this secret. When their work crowds around them more than usual they must set aside more time to pray. You can lose your power as a Christian if you don't learn this early in your Christian life. Up to this point, you may not have felt you have had time to pray, but now you have realized that no one should allow this to happen.

Through prayer, negative thoughts don't have time to develop and consume your time. Prayer gives you the time you need to meditate on the world and causes you to plunge into the "why" of creation itself—then everything begins to have purpose. God's world comes alive. You see it in the sunlight, in snow piled heavily on a tree, in children playing, in the measureless stars. You hear it in laughter; in the words, "I love you." You feel it in a baby's touch. You cannot look anywhere without the feeling of being totally surrounded by God's work—the same God who has time to hear every word you pray.

Do you feel you don't know how to pray? Are you embarrassed to talk with God about certain matters? Do you not know how to turn everything that involves your life over to him? Do you feel you don't understand how your life can be more significant than it is right now? Spiritual growth comes to your life if you allow prayer to be available at all times.

There is only one way for you to pray—the way you feel you should pray. You don't need anyone to tell you when to pray. You may feel you don't pray the most effective prayer by a theologian's standards, but you know God will show you how to pray. Don't be afraid to tell God everything. Some Christians might find it hard to believe that once they are a child of God they will always be a child of God. They begin doubting and become ashamed to tell God how they feel. Other Christians have a fear of dying, but they don't want God to know about that fear. They may worry about their family, their job, debts, but they don't feel they should bring their worries to God. God wants to reassure you that you'll always be his child. He wants to know what makes you afraid, what causes you to worry. Just your praying and telling him these things will make you feel better and you will begin thinking more positively about your life and how you feel that God wants to help you.

If you have never considered mentioning everything to God in prayer try it right now. Maybe the right words won't come, but the Holy Spirit will help you. I assure you that you will have an enormous amount of relief by sharing these things with God. It becomes a spiritual therapy to be able to talk with him about things that have bothered you, possibly for years.

When to Pray

As prayer is gradually included in more of each day, you will understand that prayer is a responsibility and a joy. By staying in an intimate and immediate contact with God, you will not misuse or misunderstand God's gifts. As this growth continues, prayer will include and pervade every aspect of your existence! You will begin praying before you enter any kind of service. The Scriptures say, "Seek the Lord while you can find him. Call upon him now while he is near" (Isa. 55:6). God is telling you to be in a continual attitude of prayer. He knows the kind of world in which you are involved. He knows the things with which you will be confronted, how you will be tempted, become afraid, and at times, even doubt his supremacy. So he allows you to come to him in prayer. Think back through today. You have had many opportunities to pray. But there are those who say, "I just don't have time to pray." If you have ever felt this way in the past, I hope by the time you have finished reading this chapter, you can see there is more time than you realize.

Perhaps in the beginning prayer should begin with a planned time each day, although this certainly is not the only time a person can pray. There are many Christians who will share with you what a daily planned time with God means to their lives. For most of my life I have been in a position to hear speakers say over and over that Christians must have a daily prayer life. And yet, in my young Christian life I couldn't see how it could make that much difference.

I finally decided to begin scheduling my time to "sacrifice" five minutes each morning for prayer and reading the Bible. I had the attitude, "I probably won't be able to see that much difference, but I can at least give it a try." It took almost a month for me to see any significance in those few minutes with God. After several mornings had passed, I found that I was talking with God for much longer periods and I was astounded that he and I had so much to talk about. Today, after many years, this quiet time is as much a part of my life as getting dressed for the day.

I had put off having a quiet time with God because I felt I was still making it in life without much prayer. The day came when I felt spiritually dry—empty. I then realized I should have stopped long ago to become spiritually filled, but I just hadn't taken the time.

One of your hardest accomplishments, but by no means an impossibility in your growth as a Christian, is simply learning to sit still and think about God. During that time don't spend any of the time thinking about all the bad things that are happening. Think about God. You aren't being asked to carry the burdens of the world on your shoulders, you can't plan your own life—these are God's responsibilities.

In your noisy world you are going to have to find your quiet mountains. You may have to create them. If you have a great responsibility facing you, get away, depart from the hurry of your life, in order to rest and reflect. It is in solitude that you hear the voice of God. Everyone must have moments of withdrawal. "But when you pray, go away by yourself, all alone, and shut the door behind you and pray to your Father secretly, and your Father, who knows your secrets, will reward you" (Matt. 6:6). When you close the door to pray, you must also discipline your mind to shut out the noise. You must be able to disregard any distractions so that this time is yours and God's.

When our children were small, we lived in a house that had a large walk-in closet. I had never thought it could turn out to be a place of prayer, but there comes a time that some place has to become a place of prayer. One evening I was unusually tired and knew I wanted to pray, not about any specific matter, but I just wanted to pray. I asked my husband to watch the children. He urged them into the family room so they wouldn't see where I was going. I opened the closet, found a small stool, and turned on the light. Then I proceeded to put a towel at the bottom of the door so the children couldn't see the light shining under it. Then God and I had some time together. I still don't remember what I talked over with him, but I remember that night and I was satisfied I had gotten to be alone with God and talk with him.

The practice of stillness and being alone with God will give you strength to endure frustrations and uncertainties. You cannot listen to your own thoughts if you are not in a state of *stillness,* a word almost extinct to this generation. In listening to your thoughts, you can learn more about your inner needs. If this idea sounds foreign to you, spend just a short period of time each day familiarizing yourself with your thoughts. Discipline your mind to spend the entire time on just that. By retreating from your pattern of living, you begin to cultivate your thoughts and the desires that gnaw at you day after day until they are perfected and satisfied.

I have known people who have said that most of their adult life they have wanted to accomplish a particular thing but they've never found the time to develop that desire. God gives each of us one life. Therefore, if each person feels deeply enough to accomplish something different with his life, then it's time to start talking with God about it. Why not take a walk, relax at home or in an empty church building, or indulge in the quiet atmosphere of a public library. Tell God that without fully realizing it, you have been caught up in a vicious circle of hurrying through this life. In your talking with God ask him to give you a calm spirit. Don't become impatient with this request. If you have followed a hectic schedule for a long time, it may take awhile to feel calm. Tell God that even though you can't get away from your daily routine for very long at a time, you would like for him to help you stop long enough to just look at the beauty that surrounds you.

By seeking solitude you will provide yourself with an opportunity to become comfortable with your feelings and thoughts, and you will begin to assess the strategies for reaching your objectives. This time may be a very honest, searching time for you as you accept the realization that you might possibly have limited yourself by not creating any specific goals. This in itself would make your quiet time valuable.

Jesus had his quiet times, his times of unhurried prayer. He prayed when there was a need to pray. His prayer life serves as an example to us. Simplicity was important in Jesus' life. Unfortunately, the world does not cling to simple things. Being aware of this helps you concentrate harder on making simplicity become a significant part of your daily goals.

Meditate. God doesn't want you to be so busy that you can't learn about him and what he freely offers you. Learn to totally absorb your thoughts in the greatness of God. If you have not taken advantage of this practice and you feel God cannot possibly supply all your needs, then you are limiting God in your life.

How do you get out of the routine of the day in order to feel alone, to have time to think? First, you must believe it will benefit your life and that it can help change your direction. The importance of a quiet time is what you gain from the experience of being alone with God. Someone has said that we discover ourselves bit by bit in the quiet moments when earth pauses and we are still.

John Kieran said:

> The last thing I do every night before I go to bed is to step out on the front lawn and look upward. If it's raining or snowing, I like to feel it on my face. If the moon is in the sky I love to look at it. If it's a moonless clear night, with a sparkling array of stars I take delight in watching the slow westward circling of the great constellations that make the ceaseless changes of the seasons in our clime. There is always something old to be sought and enjoyed, always something to be found and treasured.

God's silence. How peaceful to be a part of it, to have it revealed in most glorious ways, and to claim just a portion of it in the solitude of his presence.

There will be many times to have planned prayers. You will feel a need to start or end your day with a definite time set aside just for that. Many people contend that to pray at all, a person must pray at a certain time—once a day. This is commendable and possibly necessary for many if they feel they may not pray otherwise. But what about people who find it difficult or next to impossible, waiting for a quiet time to come? The Scriptures say, "Pray without ceasing" (1 Thess. 5:17, KJV).

There will come a time, if it hasn't already, that you will need to pray as often as you breathe. God wants you to pray while you are going about your work. He wants you to express your thanksgiving for the physical capacity to be able to do your work, and for the mental facilities to plan, to create, and to fulfill. God wants you to become comfortable with prayer. He wants it to become so natural that you find yourself praying no matter where you are or what the circumstances might be. Nothing can block out God's voice when he is speaking and you are willing to listen and respond. If you are facing a busy day, tell God; but also let him know that even in your busyness, you will talk with him and stay in contact. Begin practicing and disciplining yourself to be aware of God's presence in every aspect of each day. You will be amazed at the turn your life will take.

God is completely aware of all the things with which you are confronted. He knows how you will react, knowing it is your human nature to become discouraged, to be impatient, to criticize. In all these times he is trying to help you become aware that there are things in your life that must be removed. His solution to all these things is for you to keep on asking and it will be given to you; keep on seeking and you will find; keep on knocking and the door will be opened. (See Matt. 7:7.) By doing this your life can be cleansed through prayer and become suitable for use in a greater way. By seeking him first, you refuse to ask for or seek to gain anything selfishly.

It could be that society has caused you to believe that if you aren't busy, rushing, pushing, doing, then you're not accomplishing. When all the activity in your day makes you feel you have no way to contact God, your day has become too complicated. It is your fault, not God's. You may have to defy the pressures of civic clubs, social prominence, business status, family demands, and even recreational activities. You may have to give up some of these things, even though you find pleasure in all of them, in order for you to recharge your life. God doesn't ask you to give up everything that you enjoy. He just doesn't want you to make the mistake of neglecting to receive his spiritual healing that comes through prayer.

Praying for Others

You have felt God's power when you have had a need and you prayed about it. There is also a spiritual significance in praying for other people. Jesus has said, "When others are happy, be happy with them. If they are sad, share their sorrow" (Rom. 12:15). "Share each other's troubles and problems and so obey our Lord's command" (Gal. 6:2).

When you have an infection, your doctor may decide to give you an injection. This injection is given in a part of your body away from the infection. Then the medicine spreads its healing power to the infected area. God can take prayers offered in one place and spread their healing benefits to the "diseased" areas of others' lives.

When a person's name comes to your mind, you probably do not know that one's specific need but God does. So immediately lift that person's name in prayer. Take advantage of every prayer situation. Pray for the people you read about in the newspaper, for society's pacesetters, for national leaders, for doctors, and for schoolteachers.

When children leave home, parents can no longer reach out and touch them, hear their voices, or know of their needs, but interceding in their behalf can mean all the difference in their lives. One day as I was doing my housework, I suddenly thought of our daughter at college. I simply prayed that God would give her physical safety for the day. Later when she came home for a visit, she related a happening that occurred the very day I had prayed for her safety. She had been working with a sharp instrument in an art class. The knife slipped and cut her wrist next to a large vein. Coincidence? I believe that God foresaw a need in her life and prayer interceded for her and saw her safely through that hour.

Another evening I was not able to sleep. I began thinking about my sister. I told God I didn't know her needs but I knew he did, so I mentioned her in prayer. I found out later she had been up most of the night, the same night I had prayed, talking to one of her children about a very serious problem.

You have had friends going through extremely trying times with failing health, financial stress, family problems, or unbearable sorrow, but even though you are away from them, you can pray. "Keep praying earnestly for all Christians everywhere" (Eph. 6:18b). You cannot possibly know the force your prayers have on other lives, but they do because God promised: "Pray much for others; plead for God's mercy upon them; give thanks for all he is going to do for them" (1 Tim. 2:1). By verbally expressing this area of your prayer life, you are capable of being a part of the miracles God still performs in the lives of those whom he creates. And when you have prayed for another person "Expect God to act! For I know that I shall again have plenty of reason to praise him for all that he will do. He is my help! He is my God!" (Ps. 42:11).

Asking in Prayer

There will be times in your life when your needs will go beyond your human resources. When this happens remember this promise: "You can ask him for anything, using my name, and I will do it, for this will bring praise to the Father because of what I, the Son, will do for you" (John 14:13). Have you ever asked Jesus to heal your hurts, to make you a better person, to help you understand yourself and others, to give you wisdom, patience, or to renew a right spirit within you? There is nothing selfish when you pray for things in Jesus' name. When you pray "in Jesus' name," you are saying: "If it's what you want, if it goes along with the purpose you have for me, and if it means your and my working together, let's do it."

As you begin to pray, ask God to control your prayers. Let him know you are open to learn everything there is to know about prayer. If it will help you to become a more unselfish person, you're willing. If it allows you to be more truthful to yourself and others, you're ready. If it will keep you from worrying, he will show you how even that can be removed from your life.

By talking to God openly, he is going to reveal hidden needs in your life that you were unaware of until you began to pray. Since he already knows your needs, he can reveal them to you. For "Your Father knows exactly what you need even before you ask him" (Matt. 6:8). You may ask the question, "If God already knows these needs why should I bother to mention them in prayer?" A psychiatrist encourages his patients to talk. If the patient will be honest and open with himself and will talk freely, he will learn a great deal about himself and what might be bothering him — things that have been hidden for a long time may come to the surface if they are talked about. In talking with God, be open with him so he will be able to help you.

As you pray, ask God to teach you how to serve him and how to be willing to follow his plan for your life, how to be persistent even in the midst of unplanned circumstances, working through them with his help. God has said, "He will keep in

70

perfect peace all those who trust him, whose thoughts turn often to the Lord!" (Isa. 26:3). What causes you to lose your peace? Is it debts, guilt, your health? God promises "perfect peace" as long as your mind and your thinking is with him.

Confessing in Prayer

The day you met Christ, you confessed your need for him in your life. Remember that Jesus expects you to continue confessing to him. You made a confession to God the day you became a Christian, but you must return again and again in confession. "If we confess our sins to him, he can be depended on to forgive us and to cleanse us from every wrong" (1 John 1:9). Confession will bring about a greater peace of mind, more than just a mind that is free from guilt. Tell God daily that you have done things in your life that grieve him, things that have not been in accordance with his plan for your life. When you do this, it keeps your soul undisturbed and you will live and work more effectively. Recognize your faults, confess them, and then God will forgive you.

In the Scriptures there is an account given about King David, "a man after [God's] own heart" (1 Sam. 13:14, KJV). But David found that one wrong act could have ruined all he possessed if he had not found it in his heart to confess his wrong to God.

David had fallen in love with Bathsheba, another man's wife. He saw her beauty and immediately he wanted her. He requested that she be brought to him. In this adulterous act, Bathsheba became pregnant. David immediately sent for Uriah, Bathsheba's husband, who was away fighting in a war. Upon his arrival, David suggested that while Uriah was home that he should go to be with his wife. Uriah did not yield to the king's wishes. He felt he would be doing the other soldiers an injustice if he went home when they could not. Because of

Giving God What You Are

Uriah's decision, David could not hide his sin.

He began thinking about how to get rid of Uriah. He ordered him to the front lines of battle where Uriah was killed. After the mourning time was over, David sent for Bathsheba. He took her as his wife and began to live with the consequences of his sin. It was a long time before David permitted himself to face up to what he had done.

David's sin had not only hurt him but it had involved Uriah, Bathsheba, and the people David ruled. But God was hurt more than anyone because David's sin had been a rebellion against God's will, and this act showed a rejection of God.

David appealed directly to God and begged him for mercy. There was no way to turn but to God, and, as only God can and does, he was there to accept David's genuine confession. In his prayer of confession in Psalm 51 David begged God to hide his face from his sins. He knew God could make everything right and that this request was a tribute to God.

David had brought himself to face up to his own weaknesses. He could not stand the thought of being separated from God, and so he asked God to restore the joy of his salvation. He knew only God could bring about this healing.

Being a king did not give David any special privileges when it came to sinning. His social and political prominence didn't mean anything as far as God was concerned.

Consider the importance of daily confession in your prayer life. God knows the seriousness of it and that is why he tells everyone to cleanse their lives daily. He wants a wrong offered up in such a way that he can straighten it out and make it right. You may have trouble forgiving yourself, even after you have confessed to God, but understand this—after your confession, God emphatically, once and for all, forgets that sin.

God uses the confessions of men in the Scriptures that could be used as guidelines for others' confessions. "Search me, O God, and know my heart; test my thoughts. Point out anything you find in me that makes you sad, and lead me along the path of everlasting life" (Ps. 139:23-24). "How can I ever know what sins are lurking in my heart? Cleanse me from these hidden faults. And keep me from deliberate wrongs; help me to stop doing them. Only then can I be free of guilt and innocent of some great crime" (Ps. 19:12-13).

At least twice a day empty your mind of all your fears, uncertainties, selfishness, impatience, misunderstandings, unjust criticisms, unhealthy desires, envies, and busyness. With all of these taking up so much room in your life, Christ is allowed very little space to dwell within your life. You want him to have sufficient room to help you grow, produce, succeed, and experience the beauty of your life and the goodness of other people.

Concentrate on emptying yourself completely of my accomplishments, my talents, my desires, so that the love of God cannot help coming in and filling that big emptiness. Enable God to be the only God in your life.

You may consider praying a similar prayer of confession as this one: "Lord, I allowed so many wrong things to come into my life yesterday. I have already done things today I'm ashamed of; should you allow me to see tomorrow, I know other things will come into my life that shouldn't be there. Cleanse me, empty my life so you'll have room to come in and dwell with me. Amen."

Praising God in Prayer

I have been so happy after praying a prayer of confession that I've wanted to find a large field away from everything and everyone and shout as loud as I can to this Lord that is real, living, healing, forgiving, and performing miracles in my life.

At these times, there is no way you can keep from expressing your happiness in the Lord. Your soul will have longings you can't explain. You feel it so deeply that all you can do is praise God. You want to honor his existence, his greatness, his magnificent love, his perfectness. You want to thank him for always being with you in times of need and for using all circumstances for changing your heart and your attitudes.

As you praise God, you don't have time to think about all your obligations and your daily routines. Now you have a chance to renew your relationship with God so you won't miss for one day having that daily refreshing walk with him. Sharing your joys with God are some of the greatest experiences you will ever have in prayer. Let God know that even though this world you live in is faced with incurable diseases, broken homes, moral decline, political upsets—even with all these things you realize God created the world to be a beautiful place. Thank him that right in the middle of all this chaos he can touch your life with peace.

The more you learn about God, the more time you will be taking to praise him in your prayer life. You will be surprised that you won't be asking God for nearly so many things. The things you need will be provided. You have more time, therefore, to praise God. Some of the most meaningful encounters you will ever have with God will be when your thoughts are only about him. You will completely forget about yourself during those moments. It is easy to forget all about the things that went wrong today when you start to think about the blessings of your day. You have a family that loves you, you are surrounded by friends, you have your health. You have a house that meets your needs, you have transportation available. You have your mental faculties, you can walk, run, sing, smile, have someone hug you, and hear someone say, "I appreciate you."

When the wind touches your face, God is there. When you see children playing, God is there. When you watch birds and squirrels finding daily food, when you see the lights in a home after dark, and when you see the stars, God is there. You can feel the soft grass in springtime and smell the fragrance of a garden, the fresh dirt, or cut timber. You can stand in complete silence on a winter's day and see a stream trickling through the snow. "Oh, God, even when some of these benefits are not mine, may I continue to praise the glories of your work in other ways."

Thanking God in Prayer

You have been with God in your quiet moments of prayer and you have been with him during an unusually busy day. The awareness that you can pray to God at any time, no matter where you are or what you might be doing, makes you want to take every advantage to talk with him. One day it may come to you in its full light that even through all these talks with God, something might be missing—you feel you have not adequately expressed your gratitude toward him. Because your heart is so full and literally running over, you offer up your thankfulness.

Dear Lord, when I realize that you understand when no one else understands—my hurts, my frustrations, and my own unworthiness—I know I can come to you completely undone and find peace.

You have guided me through frightening experiences and helped me accept what happens in my life. You are the only one who knows my desires to live a better life and you keep

Giving God What You Are

loving me even when those desires are not fulfilled.

You know time can be my enemy, that I get uptight when I face such a busy day, and yet when I tell you about it you seem to give me the extra time I need to get things done and get them done well.

Lord, thank you for the daily elements of living. I am whole, but if there ever comes a time in my life when I am not whole, give me the faith to know you will help me become whole again, through your love. Amen.

Answers

I couldn't understand . . . I asked for wisdom.
I looked for beauty . . . I saw the mountains.
I searched for peace . . . I found a quiet place.
I yearned to be loved . . . I knew nothing
    could separate me from his love.
I felt lonely . . . I knew I had a Friend.
I was tired . . . He strengthened me.
I was in need . . . He satisfied me.
I was worried . . . He gave me faith.
I was afraid . . . I trusted him.
I needed hope . . . I knelt in prayer.
I went before a God I could not see
    and there I found the answers.

5
Listening to God

Several years ago I became acquainted with a young woman in my neighborhood. She was going through some trying times. As we visited with each other she shared with me that she was not satisfied with her life, especially with her spiritual life. She and her husband had attended church when they were first married, but when children were born into their home they felt it was too great of an effort to go to church.

One day I took her a copy of *Good News for Modern Man.* She accepted it and promised to try and find time to read it. I didn't know exactly how it would help her but I felt good about giving it to her.

Shortly after that we moved to a different community. I thought of my friend often and I wondered how she and her young family were getting along. A few years later I received this letter from her.

Dear Pat,

Do you remember that four years ago you gave me a copy of *Good News for Modern Man?* I must admit I didn't read it daily the first three years. I have had it in my possession all this time, but these past few months I've had it on the floor by my bed where I read it almost every night.

These past few months have been joyous but also I've had

many pressures that had made me feel I wasn't coping as easily as I would have liked, so I turned to God and *Good News* for help.

Everything isn't solved yet. I still worry too much, but hopefully in time, as my understanding of God increases, my worries about being a good mother and wife will decrease. I have already felt the stirrings of new strength and feel a true communication with God. I have been blessed beyond all measure because of this book.

There is no way to know how many people have read the Bible and been blessed beyond all measure because of this book. No one has ever been able to write a book to compare with it. Stories have been written from its contents, movies about it have been produced, plays have been performed, music has been created, and the story continues to remain applicable even in this sophisticated society today.

Why the Bible Is Different

This incomparable book was written by various writers over a period of fifteen hundred years in different places from Babylon to Rome. When these works were finished by those chosen to record the words of God, they were put together to tell the complete story of One whose love would wind its way through history, changing the life of every person who would accept his matchless love. These words give people the power to live and it explains to everyone who reads it the supreme purpose of their existence. This book, if it hasn't already, will become the greatest possession in your Christian life.

Alexander Duff was on board the ship *Lady Holland*. He was going to India as a missionary. He had brought all of his valuable possessions with him, including his library of eight hundred books. The ship wrecked just a short distance from the shores of India. Miraculously, all the people were saved. As the passengers stood on the shore watching the ship go down, Mr. Duff saw something floating in the water. He waded out to see what it was. It was his Bible, the only one of his eight hundred books that was saved.

A few days later, under a tree on the very spot where he had been standing when he saw his Bible in the water, he began to teach the Bible to five young boys. Soon the group grew to three hundred. Later a school was erected in that area where today hundreds of students now study the Bible and glorious changes are made in their lives because of God's Word.

A couple received a telegram that their young son, who was serving in the armed forces overseas, had been killed by lightning. That evening, as these parents sat together, they opened the Bible to the Scripture from John 11:25-26: "I am the one who raises the dead and gives them life again. Anyone who believes in me, even though he dies like anyone else, shall live again. He is given eternal life for believing in me and shall never perish."

God's Word can bring you more comfort and security than you ever thought possible. How does it make you feel when you start reading and you know these words are God's words? What a privilege to gaze upon the very words of God. You can't know everything he has promised to share with you if you don't take the time to discover what his promises are.

People do much worrying about themselves and about the future, but Jesus says, "Let him have all your worries and cares, for he is always thinking about you and watching everything that concerns you" (1 Pet. 5:7).

People become so burdened with family situations and try to get them straightened out in their own strength, but God says,

79

Giving God What You Are

"Casting all your care upon him; for he careth for you" (1 Pet. 5:7, KJV).

Christians can't understand how God can continue to love them when they have given in to their sinful nature, but the Bible states: "For I am convinced that nothing can ever separate us from his love . . . nothing will ever be able to separate us from the love of God demonstrated by our Lord Jesus Christ when he died for us" (Rom. 8:38-39).

People lose hope. God says, "No mere man has ever seen, heard or even imagined what wonderful things God has ready for those who love the Lord" (1 Cor. 2:9).

To culminate all that God is saying in these Scriptures, as well as in his entire Word, is "If you abide in me, and my words abide in you, ask whatever you will, and it shall be done for you" (John 15:7, RSV).

The Bible is one of God's ways of talking to us. The Scriptures say, "The whole Bible was given us by inspiration from God and is useful to teach us what is true and to make us realize what is wrong in our lives; it straightens us out and helps us do what is right" (2 Tim. 3:16). The word *inspiration* in this verse means "God breathing." So, God breathed into chosen human messengers, enabling them to record the words he wanted them to record. "For no prophecy recorded in the Scripture was ever thought up by the prophet himself. It was the Holy Spirit within these godly men who gave them true messages from God" (2 Pet. 1:20-21).

These facts make the Bible both divine and human; divine because it is the inspired words of God, human because God chose men who became divinely inspired and were guided and guarded so there would be no error. "For verily I say unto you, Till heaven and earth pass, one jot or one tittle shall in no wise pass from the law, till all be fulfilled" (Matt. 5:18). (Read this

80

verse from *The Amplified Bible* for clear understanding of the verse.)

You have inherited every promise in the Bible since you have become one of God's children. As you read, you learn that everything that is God's is yours. If you don't read it there is no way for you to know all that is given to you in your Christian life. Try to understand that if you do not search the Scriptures you will never know how God can help you in any situation. You will struggle alone and try so hard to uncomplicate your life when all that is necessary is that you turn everything over to God.

People do much talking, but they need to concentrate more on listening—especially listening to God and what he has to say about their lives. Putting yourself into a frame of mind to listen to God requires much discipline. How many times have you gone to God in prayer and felt you did all the talking? It would be the same principle as going to visit someone and having them do all the talking. There might have been some thoughts you would have liked to insert, but you never had the opportunity. Give God time to speak. His Word tells you to "Stand Silent! Know that I am God!" (Ps. 46:10).

The Bible Is Your Guide

The Bible is the Christian's guide. It tells you how to regulate your life, how to conduct your activities, how to speak to and live with others. You can read books written by Christians and they may help you grow stronger in your faith, but always go back to the Scriptures for your final authority. When you go to a strange land that requires a guide you know that the guide isn't going to carry you to where you are headed. Instead, you will walk behind him, trusting that he will guide you in the right direction. God will not carry you through this life. But if you will walk behind him, in his steps, by following his Word, you will find the right direction.

Abraham Lincoln said, "I accept what I can of the Bible by reason. When my reason cannot comprehend it, I go by faith until my reason catches up with my faith." Accept the fact that the Bible is God's message to you. Understand that it can help you with every circumstance you experience, every emotion you express, every thought you have, and every action you perform. The Bible has the power to change your attitudes, your thoughts, and your direction. If you will allow it, the Bible can't help but become an integral part of your daily spiritual life.

My husband had gone back to seminary to obtain his doctoral degree. We had prayed about the matter because it would possibly create some financial problems for us. After arriving on campus and getting settled in our apartment, I went through the process of filling out forms for substitute teaching in order to help with the income. The person in charge of securing substitute teachers for the city assured me there would be plenty of work. He told me that when a regular teacher needed a replacement, he would call no later than 10:00 the night before and let me know to which school I was being assigned. My husband had an office job in conjunction with his study program, and later hoped to have a weekend pastorate.

Each night I would stay up faithfully until 10:00. There were no calls. A month went by. There were still no calls. In my anxiety I prayed: "Lord, when we came here, we came believing this is what you wanted us to do. I promised you I would be willing to work in order for my husband to receive his education. I have waited for work, but nothing is available. Please assure me that we have made the right move. Amen."

Listening to God

The night I prayed was the same day my husband had received a call to preach in a small country church quite a distance from the seminary campus. It was late when he got home and I had already gone to bed.

The next morning I got up early to plan my weekly menus. I looked in the refrigerator freezer to see how much meat I would have to buy for the week. I couldn't believe it! The freezer was full of freshly packaged meats and vegetables from one of the farmers who attended the church where my husband had preached the day before.

I closed the refrigerator door. I thanked God, and in my thanksgiving I accepted this verse in his Word, "But my God shall supply all your need according to his riches in glory by Christ Jesus" (Phil. 4:19, KJV). He did just what he promised he would do. In just a matter of weeks my husband accepted an invitation to a regular weekend church and I received my first job to substitute teach. I began receiving calls every day to teach. It was a hard job, but God granted me this opportunity in order to help care for our family while preparing for greater fields of service. Once more the Scriptures had renewed my faith. I accepted, by faith, that our needs would always be met.

When you became a Christian and you knew God had forgiven all your sins, you had a moment of great relief. You will learn more about that forgiving power as you read about it in the Bible. You knew by the grace of God that you were able to accept Jesus as your personal Savior. As you continue to read about his grace you will understand more fully what he meant when he said: "My grace is sufficient for thee" (2 Cor. 12:9a, KJV). If you continue reading the Scriptures and learning about his love you will realize it cannot be compared to any earthly love you have ever known. When you feel you have comprehended compassion and then read about Jesus' compassion you will realize you possess only the fragments of the full meaning of compassion.

Learn to Read the Bible Daily

Have you felt a twinge of negligence for not reading God's Word more diligently? Do you feel that your days are so full now that you can't possibly add Bible study to it? You may rationalize away the importance of it when you tell yourself that you will start when you have some extra time. In all probability the extra time will never produce itself. The simplest way to find the time is to ask God to give you the initiative to want to study the Bible, then time won't be a problem with you.

What time of day are you at your best, physically and mentally? Set aside three minutes of that time to read the Bible. God doesn't command you to learn more about him. This desire must come from within your life. You don't read the Bible just because another person tells you that you should. You must feel the necessity of reading it. Never underestimate this time you spend listening to God. Go expectantly—seeking and searching. "You will find me when you seek me, if you look for me in earnest" (Jer. 29:13).

Use a version of the Bible that speaks plainly to you. Be ready to respond when a verse or verses speak to you. God guides you as you read. He then has you take the message and makes it live in your life. That teaching may come later at a time not yet revealed to you. If you expose yourself to the total message, you won't be able to end that short time with God without asking him what he wants you to do and how he wants you to interpret life for that day.

You can be assured that several things will start happening

in your life that were not present before you began reading the Scriptures. You will be more at peace with yourself and others. The words you read will encourage you. You will understand that God continues to use people even when they make mistakes. Many times the Bible tells you how God used various people in biblical times, even when they made very grave mistakes. God showed he could use them in spite of their weakness, inability, unwillingness, and rebellion. He can do the same with your life.

Do small unexpected incidents of each day aggravate you? Many Christians have said that a disciplined study of the Bible helps them maintain a higher frustration level. If you are looking for no other reason than this to read the Bible, it will be invaluable to you. But perhaps the greatest value in listening to God speak to you through his Word is the insight you will get into the character of God. "How great he is! His power is absolute! His understanding is unlimited" (Ps. 147:5). He enjoys using his power to forgive, to display compassion, and to give you comfort and hope when you recognize your own helplessness and turn to him.

Receiving Strength Through the Scriptures

A young couple was told by their doctor that the husband had a terminal illness. The man would be leaving his wife to rear three young sons alone. During his illness, he and his wife continually read these simple but powerful words of God, "Let not your heart be troubled" (John 14:1a). It pleased God to be able to bring comfort to that young couple through his Word.

How do you convince yourself, if you haven't before now, that God's Word is vital, that it is to be given top priority, that it has been proved to be the infallible guide to your life? "You can never please God without faith, without depending on him. Anyone who wants to come to God must believe that there is a God and that he rewards those who sincerely look for him (Heb. 11:6). And what kind of faith is it that this verse speaks about?

> It is the confident assurance that something we want is going to happen. It is the certainty that what we hope for is waiting for us, even though we cannot see it up ahead. By faith—by believing God—we know that the world and the stars—in fact, all things—were made at God's command; and that they were made from things that can't be seen (Heb. 11:1-3).

The kind of faith that God speaks of can only be learned by reading about it in his Word. This is the way Christians build up their spiritual reserve and prepare themselves for the things that are not yet seen in their lives.

During my teenage years the Lord saw fit to bring to our church a minister who believed, preached, and lived his Word. In God's wisdom he led that wonderful Christian man to cause me to see the importance of hiding God's word in my heart, and it was fun! He simply asked anyone who would to memorize a verse of Scripture each week and to come back to the next mid-week prayer service and quote the verse they had learned. I wanted to be one of the ones to be able to stand and quote a verse along with the older Christians. But the contest became deeper than that, and it was to continue to go even deeper through the rest of my life. Each evening I would take my Bible and sit under an old plum tree in the backyard and memorize various verses. I can remember the evenings were cool and quiet, and I was with God—listening to him.

I don't know how many verses I memorized that summer and I didn't know why I chose to memorize the ones I did, but I do now. There would be circumstances in my life that I could have never handled alone. I had hidden some of those eternal words in my heart and no one nor anything could ever remove them from my memory. "And I delight to do your will, my God, for your law is written upon my heart" (Ps. 40:8). This is how a person grows and discovers God a day at a time. There is no other guide to follow.

All people need to know and to have the kind of hope that is contained in the Bible. It contains solutions for the poor, the elite, all ages, all ranks. By believing in the authority of the Scriptures, you will want to follow the actions of Jesus. This is a magnificent expectation! It is a tremendous responsibility and an exciting opportunity!

Some people think a book is more special when it is signed by the author. When you read from the Scripture, "[He is] the author and finisher of our faith" (Heb. 12:2, KJV) it makes life special and exciting because you know God has "signed" your life, personally.

There may have been a time in your life that you thought God's Word gave only rules and condemnations, but now these same words tell you in a hundred ways that he loves you. He helps you discover the plan he has for your life through his wonderful words of life.

6
Learning About God from Other People

When I was a child I knew Saturdays would always mean something special. Occasionally I would ask Mother, "What are we going to do tonight?" She would say, "We're going to town to watch people." Which meant we would drive to town early, find a choice parking place on the main street, and watch people. We knew many of the people that walked by our car and would engage in conversation with them. Those we didn't know we would sit quietly and observe as they passed by. I can vividly remember farm families meeting each other and talking about their crops, the rains, the droughts, and their canning and gardening. The children talked about things that interested children.

I particularly remember that it was always families walking together, visiting together, and laughing together. At the time, watching people seemed a natural, normal thing to do. To my young mind it meant warm, together, and satisfying times. Today, without being too obvious and trying not to embarrass my children, I still enjoy watching people.

If I could recall all the people I saw on those Saturday nights years ago, I would see them differently now. I would know that every one of them was special to God. People are important to God. Parents, other family members, schoolteachers, friends, and brief acquaintances influence other people's lives in various ways. It would be impossible to list every person with whom you have come into contact during your lifetime. If you began to make a mental list, thinking of all those people, some of the names would remind you of happy times. Others would remind you of those people who could make you feel that you were somebody important. Others made you feel secure, complimenting you when you did something honorable; they believed in you and you knew they loved you.

If you continued your list, you might come to some names you would like to omit because they bring to mind fear, doubt, deception, frustration, jealousy, injustice, or hatred. You might want to block these people from your mind, but they are just as real to you as those who loved you and made you feel your worth.

You cannot exclude certain people from your life and expect to have many, if any, personal growth experiences. You have some private encounters between yourself and God but being with other people gives you experiences that further your growth. Impressions are made, values are questioned, and new and meaningful relationships are formed.

Learning from All Types of People

God has designed people to relate to each other. I believe emphatically that without all kinds of people being included in your life, you cannot experience continuous growth. God knows you have specific needs for other people in your life to help you be a stronger, more complete person. Naturally, you would like all of your encounters to be pleasant ones, but life hands you all types of personalities. Every life, as imperfect as it is, will play a part in cultivating your Christian life.

Some of the people you meet may come from a totally different environment than yours. Their financial status may be higher or lower than yours. They may be famous people or unknown. You may come into contact with kind, sensitive people, or with some who have built up such strong barriers that you feel that neither your love nor God's love for them could ever be strong enough to break through their veneer of hatred and hopelessness. Some people may differ from you, and you might feel it wouldn't matter if you get to know them or not. Actually, you may find yourself thinking that you don't want to know them because they couldn't add one meaningful, positive thing to your life. But stop, no matter how different these people are—their life-styles, their morals, their goals, their beliefs—they have a basic need for God just as you have. In order to face the reality of living, you cannot expect every encounter with each person to be a pleasant one, but each encounter, whether pleasant or not, can be a growing experience for you.

Many of these people will be experiencing similar things as you are in their Christian journey. They will be searching to know more about God, trying to understand him, and at intervals they, too, will have their doubting times—doubting God's power, his sovereignty over the universe, his daily presence, even doubting the words that involve God's eternal promises. You will inevitably become acquainted with at least one "doubting" Thomas, but even an acquaintance such as this could prove to be a strength when you come face to face with your own doubts.

There was a time in Thomas's life when he had to be alone and think. He had personally witnessed Jesus' crucifixion and the mental pain he experienced wouldn't release its hold on him. He kept recalling memories of the kind words of Jesus, thoughts of his broken and bleeding body, and nightmares of what had been done to the Son of God—that is, if he was the

Learning About God from Other People

Son of God. He couldn't sleep, he kept trying to recall all the words Jesus had told him and the other disciples. He felt guilty, but he couldn't keep from wondering that if Jesus were the Son of God, why had God not done something to save him from his suffering and his death on the cross? When he could face the agonizing scene no longer, he pressed his thoughts further back to the Feast of the Passover. It was then, Thomas recalled, that Jesus began talking with them in a way that Thomas could not understand. Jesus told them that he was going away, and before he could explain what he meant, Thomas interrupted and asked, "Lord, we don't know where you're going; how can we know the way to get there?" Before he had asked that question, the room had been charged with excitement and anticipation; after Thomas's untimely question, the moment lost its meaning.

All of these memories flooded into Thomas's mind as he sat recalling the events of the past three days. He had heard an almost unbelievable report earlier in the day. Some of the disciples had sent word to him that Jesus had risen from the grave! Even though it seemed impossible, the idea intrigued Thomas. He got up slowly and headed toward Jerusalem. A few minutes later he knocked lightly on the locked door that led into the room where the rest of the disciples were. When he entered the room, the disciples began telling him excitedly what had happened earlier that evening. He couldn't understand what they were saying; they were all talking at the same time. He finally got everyone to stop talking, and he asked Peter to tell him what had happened. He couldn't believe what Peter told him—Jesus was alive! He had been in the very room they were now in, and he had talked to them. Thomas looked at the other disciples. The glow on their faces affirmed what Peter had said.

Thoughts began to rush through Thomas's mind. *These men have let their emotions get away with them and they have mistaken some vision for reality. I will not let my emotions trick me.* Then he emphatically verbalized his next thought, "If I do not see the scars of the nails in his hands, and put my finger where the nails were, and my hand in his side, I will not believe."

A week later Thomas was with his friends again. They began telling him about that Sunday just a week ago. They had all been so despondent and filled with despair. Suddenly a light filled the room and Jesus was a part of that light. The light spilled over into each of the disciples and Jesus spoke, "Peace be with you."

Oh, thought Thomas, *If that could only happen to me. I want so badly to experience what the rest have known.* The thought had hardly escaped his mind when suddenly there stood Jesus with outstretched arms, emanating love. Jesus said something, but Thomas didn't hear him. He was already at the feet of Jesus, worshiping him and declaring, "My Lord and my God."

God used the lives of the other disciples to help Thomas through his time of doubting. God will inject different people into your life, also. There will be those who transmit to you that everything about life is pointless, that there is no use to strive for perfection, that to please God is an impossible goal, and that you're wasting your time. There will be others who will search out your weaknesses and get you to give up or give in to your new Christian joys. Subtly, these same people will paralyze the new hope you have found, and diminish your life in such a way that it could cripple the joy and growth of your salvation.

But what about the other people? The ones that God gives

you to improve your life? The ones who will be your encouragers, your stabilizers, your healers? The ones who will counteract all the negative reactions that others produce and will help you to have the continual belief that your Christian life does matter, that you do have the ability to make your life better than it has been today?

These people have plunged deeply into the Christian life, have seen that it is good, and have accepted God's promises that will enable them to stand against all things. Some of these people will be quiet people who have their hearts tuned to those fragile moments during your greatest needs. They will turn their complete attention toward you and their only desire will be to help you through varying experiences in your life. These people look at life enthusiastically, positively. They are happy, friendly, and thoughtful.

Don't spend one minute believing that these people aren't experiencing, and haven't experienced, "growing-up" times, too. In the face of severe adversities they have learned and are still learning to accept by faith that God is real, living, loving, and understanding. They have realized that people aren't to blame God for every wrong in the world. They can tell you that it's all right to grieve, to cry when you are disappointed, hurt, or frustrated, and let you know by the way they live that God does bear everyone up through all things. They will be willing to share similar experiences that they have gone through, and they will let you know how they have remained victorious through it all.

This chapter will be different from preceding chapters. Until now, each chapter has dealt with God or with you and your relationship to God. This chapter will deal mainly with this special group of people who will summon you to grow in your faith.

Giving God What You Are

You have a surplus of opportunities when you realize that God doesn't expect you to experience your Christian growth by yourself. It takes people helping other people. It takes opening up your real self, the self you are striving to be. God knows you need people to help you be renewed and to urge you to be all that you can be.

When you begin to see how God works through others' lives, it will help you realize all that is going to be waiting for you. God will use the indifferent people to produce in you patience, acceptance, endurance, and tolerance. He will use the other people to produce compassion, gratefulness, promise, fullness, and hope.

Learning from Family Members

Start with the basic fact that family members influence each member of any family. Maybe you didn't realize that spiritual lessons were being taught at the time, but as you grew older you could reflect back on some of the values that your family had that were not present in other families. You were being taught integrity, honesty, compassion, sharing, thoughtfulness, and, ultimately, love.

God must have created parents so that he could illustrate the depth of love he has for all his children. When a baby is born the first social contact he usually has is with his parents. The parents' voices are the first ones a baby hears. A baby experiences the first human touch from them. When a baby's eyes begin to focus, he sees his parents for the first time. Within these first experiences of seeing, hearing, and touching, a baby feels content. A baby doesn't know what love is, but what he's feeling is certainly pleasant.

It could be that you did not have a particularly happy childhood. You may have experienced more turmoil than love, more rejection than acceptance. If this is so, read the following pages carefully and prayerfully, and be determined that with God's help you will be able to create spiritual happenings of Christian love in your own home that will strengthen your children and introduce them to the teachings of Jesus.

Parental teachings and beliefs about living one's life to please God are such integral parts of some parents lives that they are blended naturally into everything they do. Because of them, if this is true of your parents, you realized that Christianity includes all of life rather than something you heard and learned about on Sunday from someone else. The knowledge of this affected how you saw other people, what you wanted to do in your life, and how you felt God wanted you to live. It caused you to want to be the same kind of silent influence that your parents had been to you.

In Galatians 5:22 the spiritual qualities are mentioned that relate to a Spirit-filled life. If you were to take each quality separately, you might see reflected in each word an incident that has occurred during your lifetime when you could say that some of these qualities were being expressed in your parents' lives. These qualities were exemplified in such a natural way that you simply accepted them as a normal part of your life. For instance, the first "fruit," *love*. Parents have a natural instinct for earthly sacrificial love which is easily related to God's sacrificial love.

I can remember a specific incident in my life when my mother exemplified sacrificial love. I could not have called it that at the time, but I know today that's what it was. This incident happened many years ago, after I had been selected pianist for our church youth group. I would practice the songs all week and on Sunday my trembling hands would miss every other note.

Giving God What You Are

As I became more confident playing the piano, I was asked to accompany a group at the church Christmas program. I still remember the two songs I was asked to play, "Silent Night," because it was easy, and "More Like the Master," because it had some difficult notes to play at the end of the verse. I practiced diligently, but on the Sunday afternoon before the program that night it began snowing and sleeting. My parents told me that if it got much worse we wouldn't be able to go. I remember feeling disappointed, but in those days a child didn't keep asking, "But why?" As it got later, the weather was no better. Mother came to me and said, "If we dress up warm and start early enough, you and I will walk to the church." We lived a mile away, but it didn't seem far when she told me I'd get to go. I don't recall much about playing the piano that evening, except that I did get through the hard part of that one song. I do remember walking to church with Mother. It was a very quiet, cold night and we hardly talked all the way. When we came to one of the street lights I glanced over at Mother and all my young heart felt was love for someone who could have stayed in a warm house that night, but instead chose to help me fulfill a desire I wanted to accomplish so badly.

In later years, that evening was to remind me of the sacrificial love that parents unselfishly relinquish to their children, and the song "More Like the Master" had to mean my mother that night. I know now that love isn't always convenient, it takes time, but its meaning lasts forever.

Recreate in your mind the first stirrings you felt within your own life after your parents helped you understand love. The things they have done for you are proof that God does live through other people because he lives through your parents. Think of how your parents continued to love you during all the stages of your life. Remember when you took a long look at your hands and feet one day and you were sure they must have belonged to someone else because they surely didn't fit your body. As far as you were concerned, the word *coordination* didn't exist, but your parents kept loving you. Do you recall spending hours getting ready to go somewhere with the family? You would take your time, making sure you looked perfect, unaware that you were making everyone late. You'd go out the door and see your parents patiently sitting in the car, waiting for your appearance, and they kept loving you. How about when you came in much too late and through Mother's tears and Dad's anger, you knew it was time to have a talk with them? But they kept loving you. What about the time you were considering marriage? How did your parents react, or were you unable to distinguish any reaction? There is a loss felt — but they keep loving you.

God keeps loving you even though you can't fully comprehend his love. You feel this limitless love because your parents let you know that they loved you even though you couldn't fully understand it.

As you continued in the physical and social aspects of growing up, you became aware that there were times when you weren't accepted by certain social groups. You felt left out, and this would trigger a deep loneliness. But you knew you would feel accepted in your home, even if your family couldn't understand your hurts. It helped to know you were included, you were a part of something that was strongly united.

It has been mentioned in another chapter that Jesus included everyone in his love when he said, "Whosoever believeth in him" (John 3:16*b* KJV). To be included in God's love is the ultimate in belonging. My Dad had a very natural way of making me feel included in his life. Can you picture a young girl getting up at 4:00 on a Saturday morning, eating break-fast with her dad, and being out on the creek bank by sunrise to go fishing? Can you visualize two people together, not saying anything (Dad always said talking scared the fish away), but enjoying the beauty of an early summer morning? The only sound we could hear was the birds. We'd sit quietly waiting to get a bite, and when it finally happened to my line and I didn't think I could get my catch out, Dad would begin his loud shouts of encouragement and I'd finally land my fish. Then I'd look up in his face and see him smiling, because he was proud of me and also because I still hadn't enough courage to take the fish off the hook.

Dad included me in many of these special days. It would have been less bother for him to have gone fishing alone. Then he wouldn't have had to bait my hook, help me get my tangled fishing line out of a tree, reassure me there were no snakes in the fields we had to walk through, teach me how to crawl under barbed wire fences without snagging my clothes, or how to fish from a boat without upsetting it. But he did include me, he wanted to, and that was important to me.

When I look back on those times, especially when I find myself wrestling with a problem, dissatisfied with myself, expecting too much to happen too quickly, or going past my limitations, I can be assured that even during these times I can be at peace, knowing that God continues to include me in his love.

As God's teachings continue through other people, he blesses some families with brothers and sisters who learn to cooperate with each other. It would be natural to question whether brothers and sisters have any significant effect on spiritual growth, but they do. Perhaps the most lasting lesson to learn is sharing. It starts with sharing toys, then sharing a room, clothes, one phone, one bike, one car. It disciplines you to learn there are others to take into consideration, and not to have only your own selfish desires met. Many times that isn't easy to accept.

Jesus was the most unselfish sharing example of all times. He said, "Whoever loses his life for my sake will save it" (Luke 9:24a) and "some are last who will be first" (Luke 13:30b, RSV). This doesn't sound logical, but it's true, and the act of sharing sets up a principle that affects your life of giving in service to God.

Other people God uses to affect our lives are those special grandparents. I especially remember one of my grandmothers. She lived to be ninety-one, so she and I were given time to develop our love for each other. She raised ten children, and you can imagine how many grandchildren and great-grandchildren she saw come into the world. Each Christmas she gave everyone a gift. It would be a small, useful item she had bought or something she had made. It became an annual ritual for each family to go by her house on Christmas morning and exchange gifts with her. Today I can still see her handing me my gift wrapped in red tissue paper and remember how it pleased her that she could give something to everyone.

Not only did she successfully establish her own home and raise her own children, but she was always available to help with her grandchildren. Since both of my parents worked, my sister and I would stay with her until our parents got off from work. We knew she'd always be at her house when we got home from school and on special occasions she'd ration out her hot homemade bread and jelly with us.

She didn't talk to me much about her family, but one day when I was older we talked about many things that had happened through the years. I asked her how she had been able to

99

cope with all she had been through. Without any hesitation she said, "God promised to give me faith to help me through everything and he's kept his promise to me."

The last time I saw her she was in the hospital. It was right before Christmas. I knew how sick she was, but I asked her, "Grandma, are you ready for Christmas?" And she said, "I just about have everything ready." I kissed her and left. I knew there would be no more Christmases of receiving a gift from her. But I received and continue to receive from her, year after year, the gift of her simple understanding and acceptance of faith in God that has already seen me through everything, just as it did for her. When I recall her life, I know God placed her in my life to reassure me that through faith, all things are possible.

Do you have an older relative like this? If you do, seek that one out and ask them how they have reserved such an enormous amount of faith. Observe their living faith and thank God that he gave you one more life to teach you the meaning of living by faith in him.

I'm sure God united my life with a man who has been able to teach me that a simple, uncomplicated life is a prized possession. He has taught me how to enjoy life and not constantly fight against time and circumstances. He has patiently taught me how to love and accept myself. This knowledge has placed me in a relationship with God that has helped me to understand that God wants me to be able to relate all areas of my life to him.

Learning from Friends

It would be simple never to have to reach out past your home to increase your faith or for other levels of growth experiences, but there is more to be learned, more to be searched for, and more to be shared in the lives of people outside of your family. It surely occurred to God that because he designed your life to relate to other people, he would be generous in another area of your life by giving you Christian friends. These are the people who pray with you, cry with you, and feel your needs before you're able to distinguish what they are. They instinctively know when you've been working too hard and nudge you gently out of your daily routine, helping you to find some refreshing, well-deserved, relaxing moments. They sacrifice for you, uphold your name in prayer, are honest with you, and help you feel spiritually full by sharing so much of themselves with you.

Goethe said: "The world is so empty if one thinks only of mountains, rivers and cities; but to know someone who thinks and feels with us, and who, though distant is close to us in spirit, this makes the earth for us an inhabited garden." Often Jesus will make his resources available to you through Christian friends. These are the people who will understand you, listen to your hopes, help make your cares vanish, and give you reassureance.

Christian friends make you feel comfortable and let you know you can share an intimate confidence without fear of it being repeated. You won't be afraid to let them see your real self, even when you're not on top of everything or whatever situation they find you in. They are so radiant, so kind, so pleasure-bearing, that you instinctively feel when you're in their presence that they're going to be good for you. These people are gifted by the Lord to be "givers." These are the ones who encourage you to be the person God wants you to be. They display before you God's love through their lives even though they may be totally unaware they've done you so much good.

Giving God What You Are

Six weeks after our second daughter was born we were to move to another town where my husband was to begin a new job. He had gone two weeks earlier to rent us a house. He came home with a diagram of the house that he had rented. I sketched in where I wanted the furniture to be placed, since I would not be able to go to the new location for several days. I took our oldest daughter and the baby to a friend's house and stayed there until the moving was completed. When my husband arrived at the new location with the furniture, he asked a woman who had been a friend of our family for years to help him put things away. When I arrived a week later, not only was the furniture exactly placed but the beds were made, the dishes were in the cabinets, the utensils were in the proper drawers, the clothes were hanging in the closets, and the curtains were up.

Many years later I reminded this woman about that generous act and how much it had meant to a young, tired mother. She said that she didn't remember doing it. That had an even greater effect on me because I knew she had done it out of love and had asked nothing in return.

Learning from Teachers

The influence of friends presents a steady flow of lessons to be learned, not only spiritually, but morally and socially. These teachings will stay with you for a lifetime. Since you have spent several years of your life in school, try to think of the teachers that have had the most influence on your life. It wasn't always the subjects that they taught which caused you to remember them, but rather how they taught lessons other than book knowledge. Some of those teachers came into your life not only to teach you how to read, figure math problems, and spell, but, more importantly, they instilled in you honesty, integrity, and self-discipline.

Learning About God from Other People

Miss Jessie had been my dad's teacher and it was to be a special privilege for me to have her as my teacher, also. She didn't smile much, but she was kind-spoken and she was fair with all of her students. It was obvious she had no "pets" and I liked that best of all. Before I reached her grade, I couldn't see that studying for tests was all that important. I felt it was much more fun to play hopscotch, tag, or baseball at recess. One of my school friends that year was a very intelligent girl who always had her lessons prepared. We were to have a true-false test on one particular day, so I talked my friend into helping me with the answers. She would cautiously hold up one finger if a statement was true, and two fingers if it was false. It was a well planned strategy, or so I thought. The next day we received our graded papers, and at the top of my paper, Miss Jessie had written a note and had given me a zero because she had seen me cheating. The rest of the day was extremely long. The following day I was told to stand at my desk and tell the class I was sorry I had cheated. From that day on I do not remember ever cheating on another test.

The manner in which this wise teacher taught me about dishonesty was to influence me the rest of my life. I can't say I was grateful at that time for the incident, but I can now. That same year I became a Christian, and I believe that she pointed me in the right direction of repenting of something that was wrong. After that confession time in that fifth-grade room, I knew I could not disappoint my teacher again or be unfair to myself. That lesson has been carried on through my growing years as a Christian when I realize it is my best work God is asking from me. To do my best, I must prepare for it and it must be *my* work, *my* commitment, and *my* service.

Miss Jessie taught me honesty with myself, but Mr. Mason was to touch my life in a totally different way. Most band directors would show mercy and accept excuses sometimes, but not Mr. Mason. When he told the band to be on the football field at 8:15 AM, he didn't mean that we were to be walking to the field at that time but that we were to be ready to march at that time. He insisted everyone wear rubber boots so our feet wouldn't get wet. That sounds simple, but not when the rubber boots of all the band members were placed in two huge cardboard boxes every day after band practice. At the exact time the band lined up at the goal post, waited for a signal from the drum major, and the marching began. We were instructed to always step on each white line of the football field after six steps, with the right foot. I never missed one white line, and I remember why. Our band director carried a paddle in his hand, and he marched in and out of the rows and anyone who didn't step on a white line with the right foot after six steps got a firm swat with that paddle.

I couldn't laugh about that method of teaching for several years because it was too close to me. But I learned discipline in every sense of the word, and I knew what it meant to put everything I had into marching. We had a top-rated band, and although the teaching techniques would not meet today's standards, it taught me that strict discipline could create a desire to do better things, to do them right, and to take pleasure in going beyond what I thought might have, otherwise, been impossible.

People. There are some you meet briefly, who influence you by what they say or don't say to you. Others enter your life to experience special occasions with you, and because of this meeting, they leave a portion of their lives with you. How do you value the people whom you know believe without a doubt in you and in what you are doing? Or those who have written you and tried to express what you've meant to their lives? There are authors of books whom you'll probably never meet, but whose words have lifted your spiritual life to new heights. There are physicians who have renewed your hope through healing. There are teachers who have encouraged you to develop the gifts which have been endowed to you from God. There are musicians who have created melodies and lyrics to help you express the depths of love that could not otherwise have been expressed. There are ministers who stand before you and lead you into a personal worship with God and who exemplify the high calling of God in their daily living.

God has given you people who have genuine interest in and love for others. They have displayed such kindness that it is apparent they have projected into their lives Jesus' words, "As ye have done it unto one of the least of these my brethren, ye have done it unto me" (Matt. 25:40, KJV). Look at every person, love them, help them, value them, and in these ways you are doing it as though you are doing it unto God.

"God, I pray that you will make me aware that you are the living Savior of all people—not just for me. Help me dismiss from my life the unfairness that society, of which I am an active part, brings upon people. Help me love each person equally. Help me love them, even when I don't understand why they live the way they do. Give me the wisdom to be able to appreciate the rights and privileges of other people.

"Thank you for all the people you have placed in my life. Because of them, they have helped me see and know more clearly the one who created people for the purpose of revealing more of himself to me and to the world. Amen."

7
Walking with God "Through the Fire"

Carliss is a Christian. He has cerebral palsy. He was not able to walk until he was six years old. It was difficult for him even then, but each time he fell he would get up and try again. His speech was so poor that only his mother could understand him. Because of his condition, his skull tried to separate and he had to wear a band around his head to keep it from literally falling apart. His head was very large and so heavy that he could not hold it up straight.

The saliva poured from his moth constantly. His mother purchased some oilcloth and made him an apron to protect his clothing. When Carliss was eight years old, he began to have what was at first thought to be epileptic attacks. He took daily medication for this for thirteen years. It was finally discovered that the attacks were being caused by pressure on his brain caused by the headband he wore.

During this time he began questioning his mother about school. He began to beg to go, even when everyone told him he couldn't. When he was twelve years old, his mother could stand his begging no longer. She dressed him and sent him to school. She hoped he could at least learn to read and write so he could get some enjoyment from life. His teacher took an immediate interest in him, and he began to learn. By the time he was fifteen years old, he had reached the third grade.

Walking with God "Through the Fire"

In his early childhood he had been taught to believe in God and to love him. During his fifteenth year, he gave his life to Jesus. When he went home from church that night, he prayed for the first time, "Lord, my life seems so hopeless. I'm getting older and if something doesn't change I'm going to be a burden to my parents the rest of my life. If you'll take my life and make something out of it, I'll talk for you and glorify you the rest of my life. If this cannot be, please take my life away so I will no longer be a burden to anyone."

Things began to happen after that night. Carliss began to talk more distinctly. The continuous flow of saliva ceased, and his head began to assume a normal shape. He no longer had to make visits to the doctor, and his medicine was eventually stopped. He began making superior grades in school and sometimes would finish a year's study in two or three months. When he finished elementary school, he said he was going to high school. His friends thought he was foolish, but he had faith in God and knew he would go.

One day he discovered a verse in the Bible which he literally built his life around. "For I can do everything God asks me to with the help of Christ who gives me the strength and power" (Phil. 4:13).

He did go to high school and he finished near the top of his class. After that accomplishment he wanted to go to college. His parents were not financially able to send him, so Carliss prayed, "Lord, don't let me down now, I want to go to college." Things began to happen. Money began to come in. People he had never met began sending money to him.

The day came when he packed his suitcase and walked away from his home for the first time. While he was at college, he remembered the promise he had made to the Lord that he would talk for him the rest of his life.

Giving God What You Are

One night one of his closest friends came to him. He was very troubled, so Carliss talked with him. Before the friend left the room, he had given his life to Jesus. On another night Carliss was walking home and a policeman picked him up because he thought Carliss was drunk by the way he walked. When the policeman saw that he wasn't drunk, he started to dismiss him. But Carliss said, "Since I'm already in the car, why don't you just take me home?" On the way he told the policeman about the love of Christ, and the man was saved.

Carliss finished college and got a good job. When he told his friends that he'd like to have a girlfriend, get married, and have his own home, they advised him against it because of his affliction.

Carliss prayed, "Lord, you've given me so many things. Nothing is impossible for you. Would you find me a good girl who will love me and be happy with me, in spite of my affliction?" Within three months he met a girl and began to date her. Seven months later, they were married. They were advised not to have children because they, too, might also be affected physically. But through the years the Lord blessed that home with five normal, healthy, lovely daughters.

Carliss continues to keep his promise to God and spends his days traveling and speaking for him. He has been able to do it all through Christ. "How we thank you, Lord! Your mighty miracles give proof that you care (Ps. 75:1).

How have people like Carliss who have had incredible odds against them physically throughout their lives been able to maintain their faith in God and believe without doubting that God's grace and power are sufficient? Helen Keller said, "I thank God for my handicaps, for through my handicaps I've found my life, my work, and my God." Even through her life of total darkness and silence she believed in and accepted

108

through faith the God she could not see.

Every person is acquainted with grief. This not only includes grief through death but includes all the problems and sorrows that people must confront. No one plans to have a sudden illness that may result in a premature death. They don't anticipate divorce, birth defects, accidents, or surgery. This chapter will introduce you to various people who have been willing to share events such as these from their lives that confirmed their faith in God. They know he has been with them, because he, too, was "a man of sorrows, acquainted with bitterest grief" (Isa. 53:3).

Consider the Scripture passage: "When thou walkest through the fire, thou shalt not be burned; neither shall the flame kindle upon thee" (Isa. 43:2*b*, KJV). No one is exempt from experiencing dark, hopeless hours, but each one can be refined because they can come "through the fire" and not be burned. This refining process will reproduce in them a sensitivity in consoling those whose hurts are similar to theirs. The things they had considered important will now seem insignificant. They will no longer take for granted each day health, safety, home, life, or anything else. They will develop a reverence for life, a respect for people, a daily walk and communion with God.

Walking in God's Strength

A three-year-old boy was crying because his six-month-old sister had pulled his hair. His mother explained, "Your sister din't know it hurt when she pulled your hair." His mother left the room. Soon she heard the baby crying. She went back into the room and the little boy said, "Momma, now she knows!" In the same way it is possible for someone to share their suffering with you. You can read about the physical pain caused by an accident. You can be acquainted with a person who has had an affliction for a lifetime. You can visit with a person who is facing surgery, who has lost a loved one through death, or someone who has just been told by their doctor that they have a serious illness. But until *you* are the one who is hurting, when it is *you* overcoming the handicaps of an accident, when *you* are facing surgery, when *you* are the one who has been left with a loss through death, then you begin to feel the incomparable, painful, anguish that has been experienced by so many others before you. Then you ask: "How will I ever be able to handle this? Will the pain ever go away? Can my life ever be the same? How long will I feel this loneliness? Why has this happened to me? Why, God?"

"Why, God?" is the most universal of all questions. But here you involve God with your questioning. You may assume that the happy, perfect life is having good health and a united family, being free from injury, having enough money to take care of your needs, being secure with a substantial job, being free from worry. But this ideal fantasy can never happen in an imperfect world. In the face of stark reality you must accept that the world you live in is far from ideal.

Death is inevitable, bodies get sick, marriages are destroyed, accidents occur, imperfections are prevalent because life itself is imperfect. With so many things occuring, how can a person overcome when these tragedies happen? Those who have come through the fire with God will tell you that God has assured them that he will supply all their needs, even when certain situations seem completely hopeless. They will tell you that even though you feel you cannot go another step, when your human resources have completely diminished, God is available. He has said, "As thy days, so shall thy strength be" (Deut. 33:25, KJV).

Walking with God "Through the Fire"

It is evident, then, that it is faith in God's strength that Christians rely upon when unexpected incidents occur. When they reach this point of relying completely on God, they have the "certainty that what we hope for is waiting for us, even though we cannot see it up ahead" (Heb. 11:1b).

In the Bible the writer Paul mentions many people by name who have kept their faith in God during their greatest losses, sufferings, and dark hours. He said, "These men of faith I have mentioned died without receiving all that God had promised them; but they saw it all awaiting them on ahead and were glad, for they agreed that this earth was not their real home but that they were just strangers visiting down here" (Heb. 11:13).

In updating those times it is no different. People continue to grieve, to cope, to accept, and they continue to have the faith to believe "that all that happens to us is working for our good if we love God and are fitting into his plan" (Rom. 8:28). It is not as though all things that happen are good, but out of each experience of life some good can come if you search for it.

Since God gave up everything for us, "won't he also surely give us everything else?" (Rom. 8:32b). Problems will always exist. It's how you learn to deal with them that's important. The problems are there, but instead of anguishing over them, you must deal with them, not alone, but with God. Why struggle alone when you have been given a Comforter? God wants each person to use the faith he has blessed them with, and if things get bigger than you and you've reached your capacity for working things out, God takes over if you allow him to. You can say you want God to take over, but until you put that statement into active faith you will continue trying to take control of the situation.

There is a fine line between how much strength a man has

and where he must sever that human hold and relinquish everything that is within himself, all the limitations that are his, to God. Then God takes charge and his timing, his plan, his help is always right.

A young man found himself in a life-and-death situation. He was in construction work, and by neglect, while high above the ground, he lost his footing and started to fall. Instinctively he grabbed hold of a thick cable. His hands hit a steel railing and caused him to loosen his grip for an instant. One of his legs became entangled in the cable and he was dangling in midair. His fellow workers stood by helplessly until one man realized if he didn't act immediately the young man would fall to his death. While he was climbing to rescue him, he kept encouraging the young man to hang on. He could hear him screaming, "Someone please help me. I can't hold on much longer!" When the man reached the young man, he put his arm around his waist and told him to let go of his grasp. The young man did let go with one hand and wrapped his arm aroung the rescuer's shoulder, but his other hand remained tightly gripped around the cable. The rescuer told him to let go and grab him with both arms, but the young man still didn't respond. The man hit him. He came to, blacked out, and continued to hold his grip. The man knew he would have to change his approach, so he said softly, "Please trust me. You must trust me." He looked into the man's eyes and very slowly began uncurling his fingers from the cable. The young man now had a firm grasp with both arms around the other man's shoulders. They were then lowered to the ground. Even after they were safe on the ground, the young man would not release his grasp around the shoulders of the rescuer until his fingers were pried loose one at a time.

When situations occur in your life that are bigger than you

can handle, and you feel you can't hold on any longer, and you grasp at life tightly because of your fear of falling, God is there. He's looking into your face and he's whispering, "Trust me! You must learn to trust me." If you're willing to listen to him, you'll place the trust in him that he asks for, and then you can begin to slowly release your grip. You can place your life in his arms, and he will lift you up and ease your load.

Why must some situations become so intense before a person can say, "Take over, God?" What makes each of us keep holding on when God says, "Let go, trust me. I'm here with you." Can you bring yourself to feel clearly that you are surrounded by God's arms? When life seems disturbed and unable to be straightened out, when griefs, frustrations, disappointments, or fears come, God's grip gets stronger and you can feel it. He'll keep that firm grip around you until he feels he can gradually start releasing it. Then it becomes a more gentle touch as you get your life back to the semblance of what it once was, not the same way but a new start because you've learned something while you and God walked together so closely. You know that from this day he will never let you walk through the dark valleys alone.

Walking with God Through Illness

Learning to live in faith with God is a continual growing process. It demands patience, but you know your life will continue because you have received the promise that God will be with you as you walk through the fire. God says, "Come to me and I will give you rest" (Matt. 11:28a). This might mean a refreshing pause or a way to handle your burden so that you will not feel defeated by what has happened to you.

I find that I'm always unintentionally crowding too many activities into my daily schedule. I make a list on my busiest days so I won't forget all the things I want to get done, but I have never written anything on my list about resting in between those activities. A few years ago God allowed me to have "a refreshing pause." I didn't ask him for it. I was too busy to do that, and stopping for anything would have slowed me down and kept me from accomplishing all those "good" things I was doing.

One morning after I had done some heavy housework, I felt a severe pain in my ankle. I noticed that it was swollen and discolored. I made an appointment to see my doctor who diagnosed my ailment as superficial phlebitis. I was to go home, elevate my leg, and stay off it as much as possible for ten days. I can remember wondering how everything would get done without me. It wasn't long until I had gotten enough of lying around. After a week, reading and writing no longer interested me. I thought it was time for me to be well. But my body wouldn't cooperate with my desires. Another week went by, and my ankle still hadn't healed. As was my habit, I began trying to analyze why God had done this to me. I tried to interpret what great meaning there was in making me incapacitated like this. Then, in my praying, it was revealed to me that God hadn't done this to me. I was the one who had abused my body, and now there must be a healing process that required rest. It was that simple. Then I prayed, "God, you've helped me in many ways through the years, and now I'm asking you to lead me through each day. Help me trust you during this time and let me know your presence as we go through this together."

My "refreshing pause" lasted five weeks. I did rest. I sat on our back porch and became intrigued with the flowers I had planted. I watched the sun set. At night I positioned my lounge chair so I could lie back and study the stars. I eagerly waited for the children to come home from school and tell me how their day had been. I watched them as they talked to me, and I honestly had time to listen to what they were saying. I invited people to visit, and we sat and talked.

Five weeks seemed a long time until I evaluated what I had learned during that quiet interlude in my life. Although my daily schedule continues to become crowded at times, I do not allow it to become so crowded that I don't have time to enjoy the flowers, the sky, my family, and friends. I thank God that he helped heal my body and taught me that in order to serve him fully, I must respect the body he has given me enough to care for it properly.

William Cowper wrote:

> God moves in a mysterious way
> His wonders to perform;
> He plants his footsteps in the sea
> And rides upon the storm

How do you react to daily problems at home, with your health, at your job, with friends? Problems will inevitably come. These problems may cause you to be slightly irritated for awhile, or they may be serious enough to give you a lifetime of grief. There will be frightening problems when even the safety of life may be in question.

One day a young mother found herself praying for patience. She felt confined being a mother and she had considered, in desperation, handing the baby to his father and saying; "You take him. You take care of him. I'm tired." She felt an almost overwhelming responsibility in being a mother, and yet she knew she couldn't walk away from that responsibility.

One evening she had put her baby in his walker and she was preparing to deep-fry the main dish for the evening meal. The baby was fascinated with the long electric cord of the skillet.

He quickly pulled on the cord and the skillet tipped over, spilling hot grease over his head, arms, chest, and legs. The mother's first thought was, "Babies die from less than this!"

The young family left immediately for the hospital. The baby's crying was actually a relief to hear as they drove for help. The child was put on the critical list. As the doctors and nurses worked with the child, they asked the parents to stay with him. They were shown how to mix various chemicals to drop into the baby's mouth through the night. The room was kept dark, so the parents were not aware of the extent of the burns.

The next morning the child's eyes were swollen shut. The doctor confided that he was not sure what he might find when the child's eyes opened. The mother prayed, "Oh God, if he can only see!"

They waited four days before they knew his sight had not been damaged. The baby made continuous progress and he was allowed to leave the hospital in three weeks.

It was evident that plastic surgery would have to be performed. When the doctor talked with the couple about it, they were unable to make a decision because they didn't know which method would be most effective. Shortly after they returned home from the hospital, the baby's mother read an article about a medical center in another state. The article described a new procedure for plastic surgery. The father called the center and made an appointment. Because the child was so young nothing could be done at that time, but at the age of three he had the first in a series of operations. These involved cutting away scar tissue and rearranging new skin over the damaged portions of his body. It was a frightening experience for such a small child, but he endured each operation. The operations continued over the next fourteen years.

Walking with God "Through the Fire"

A traumatic experience such as this was bound to have its effect on this Christian family. Through the years, they have been able to observe some of the changes that began taking place in their own personal lives. As they prayed, they thanked God that their son could see and that he could walk. They thanked him for every area of their child's body that wasn't burned, and that the scars he did receive had not restricted him in any way. "Then be happy, for when the way is rough, your patience has a chance to grow. So let it grow, and don't try to squirm out of your problems. For when your patience is finally in full bloom, then you will be ready for anything, strong in character, full and complete" (Jas. 1:2b-4).

Walking with God Through Disease

God doesn't intend for any grief to break your spirit so completely that it will keep you from seeing how to fulfill the purpose and plan for your life. Have you ever asked God for strength to help you achieve, but instead he made you weak so you would depend on him? Have you asked for health, but you were given sickness to develop patience?

Carol had a brief life. I'm sure she must have asked God many times to give her good health, but instead he gave her a life without good health in order for her to help others be strengthened in their faith. God did have a purpose for her life, and if she had not believed in him her trials would have been unbearable.

When Carol was nine years old, her doctor discovered that she was a severe diabetic. She learned to give herself shots with little difficulty, and this soon became a part of her daily routine. When she reached junior high level, she was elected to the cheerleading squad. However, the school officials informed her that she wouldn't be able to go to any of the out-of-

117

town games because they couldn't be responsible for her if she should have an insulin reaction. Since she was a band member, she was also told she could not travel with the band. Disgusted, she gave up cheerleading and band. The final blow came when she was not allowed to go on the annual senior class trip to another state.

Carol began to hate diabetes, and she decided it wasn't going to keep her from doing things any longer. This attitude led her to an early marriage. It didn't take her long to realize she had made a mistake. Later she became pregnant, but she was told by her doctor that her chances of giving birth to a child were very slim. She was determined to prove the doctor wrong, but she had a miscarriage and almost lost her own life. After four years of unhappiness in her marriage, she filed for divorce.

Carol felt totally alone. She was not a Christian, so she didn't feel she could turn to God to find comfort and help. She was then twenty-two years old, divorced, and her life seemed meaningless. She began working in an office at a college.

During that time she met a Christian man. After dating for a year, they were married. It was the happiest she had ever been. She and her husband moved to a new community where both of them had jobs. Everything went well during the first few months. Then on Christmas Eve Carol became very ill. She had tests and x-rays, but no problems could be detected. Much later she went to a medical center where it was found that she had ulcers.

Shortly after this Carol and her husband moved again, and she began having more problems. Her doctor decided to do exploratory surgery because some of her tests showed a malignancy, which later proved to be negative. She lost her eyesight, but the sight in one eye was restored by laser beam surgery. She began developing bone problems in one of her legs, and she had to have surgery to correct it. During her recuperation period she began to think about God and her relationship to him. She realized she had never given her life completely to God. She made that commitment to Christ one cold Sunday morning.

For two years she and her husband had been trying to adopt a child, although Carol doubted she would ever get a child because of her physical condition. While she was recovering from leg surgery, she and her husband received word that they had been approved for adoption. Soon after this they were notified that they were to have a baby girl.

When the baby was a year old, Carol had to have surgery again. She prayed earnestly that God would help her through this time since she had a baby to care for. She had been out of her cast this time for two weeks when she fell and broke a leg, an arm, and several ribs. Even through her pain she knew God understood all her needs.

Carol continued to have health problems, but she lived with them through faith. Each day she was given to live Carol enjoyed the blessings of that day. She never looked too far ahead or thought of the things that might be, for then her load would have been too heavy to bear.

She died shortly after she had written this story about her life for me to use in this book. It was my privilege to know her during the last years of her life. In the preface of a cookbook she had published, she wrote: "I have been given a simple faith, a searching mind, a soul longing for the highest fulfillment, and the strength to preserve me through trials, doubts, and fears."

As soon as Carol placed her life into God's hands, she developed a different attitude toward the uncertainty of the length of her life. She was able to share her burdens with him, burdens which she could not possibly have carried alone. She lived her life quietly and in faith; she died quietly to continue her existence with God, the provider of her strength.

Walking with God Through Death

Death will continue to be a mystery for the living. When someone we love no longer has an earthly existence it is extremely difficult to face the loss, although it is not impossible to overcome. You are subjected to daily irritations, but irritations have ways of being solved. Sickness can alter your schedule for awhile, but you know it won't be long until your body is healed. Surgery requires a recuperation time when daily routines are abandoned for awhile. An accident might completely disrupt your life-style and have an effect on an entire family. In all of these things the continuation of life, even though it is interrupted by tragic events, is a gift. But when the gift of life is removed, when that person no longer has a daily existence, how can loved ones accept the finality of that death? That physical body, that unique personality, the joy of seeing that person and hearing his laughter, the important place he had in your life no longer exists.

Then your life is completely submerged in grief, disbelief, anger, and depression. When you feel you will never be relieved of this sorrow, when the weight of grief is still in your heart, you begin slowly to accept the absence of the body of the one you had loved so deeply. And the beauty of acceptance is that along with it comes hope. What seemed so hopeless at first is now filled with hope.

How can a woman who loses her husband and son in a plane crash survive the immensity of the loss? With hope.

How can parents continue life after their small child has

died of a painful illness? With hope.

How can a mother erase the memory of seeing her husband and two sons killed in a bizarre car-racing mishap? With hope.

Christians who are left to mourn that death grieve, but they do not grieve as a person who has no hope.

> I want you to know what happens to a Christian when he dies so that when it happens, you will not be full of sorrow, as those are who have no hope. For since we believe that Jesus died and then came back to life again, we can also believe that when Jesus returns, God will bring back with him all the Christians who have died (1 Thess. 4:13-14).

When Jesus was raised from death into life, this act became every Christian's hope because it proved that life does not end when the earthly life is gone. Because God has gone through deep agony with his Son's death, he understands the grief others go through. God has shown over and over that grief can be transformed to become his instrument and can be used by him for good.

A woman shared the grief she experienced after the death of her young husband. Her husband had not been feeling well, and after a visit to the doctor it was confirmed that he had a malignancy. He was scheduled for surgery shortly afterwards. After the operation, he was told there was a 50 percent chance that all of the disease had been removed. On one of the visits to the doctor, after he had gone through the recuperation period, his wife went with him. While they were waiting for the doctor to come into his office to talk with them, the woman noticed her husband's medical record on the desk. The only words she recalled seeing were, "Patient is aware that prognosis is poor." That didn't sound like a 50 percent chance of recovery to her, so she immediately confronted the doctor when he came into the office. He was a committed Christian and a very kind person, and was understanding but honest with them. "You have between nine months and a year to live."

As they drove away from the doctor's office, the young couple stopped along the side of the road to gain control of themselves. They determined between themselves to make it a good year. They had three small sons, but they chose not to tell them about the seriousness of their father's illness. (She feels now she should have been honest with them.) The family began doing things the boys would remember—planning vacations, having picnics, going to their favorite parks.

Her husband was able to work at his job for three months. As the illness advanced, his wife began staying up with him until the early morning hours. This was extremely tiring for her, and members of her family came to help. Some of them sat with her husband and others cared for her sons. Within a few months her husband died.

The Scriptures gave this young wife strength to surrender this difficult time to God and kept her from trying to take her present circumstances into her own hands. These Scriptures comforted her during her grief:

> All who are oppressed may come to him. He is a refuge for them in their times of trouble. (Ps. 9:9).

> Let him have all your worries and cares, for he is always thinking about you and watching everything that concerns you (1 Pet. 5:7).

> What a wonderful God we have—he is the Father of our Lord Jesus Christ, the source of every mercy, and the one who so wonderfully comforts and strengthens us in our hardships and trials. And why does he do this? So that when others are troubled, needing our sympathy and encouragement, we can pass on to them this same help and comfort God has given us (2 Cor. 1:3-4).

Walking with God "Through the Fire"

After her husband's death, she moved to another location and immediately began graduate school. She continued to have faith that God would see her through the many adjustments she must make, and she continued to rely upon portions of Scripture that had sustained her and her husband throughout his illness. Her oldest son told her later that it was the death of his father that firmly established his faith in God because he was able to bear his mother up in her grief.

When this young couple repeated their marriage vows and promised to love each other "til death alone shall part you," the thought of death didn't occur to them as they planned a long lifetime together. When death did come and she committed this loss to God, he gave her a glimpse of hope and she was able to appreciate the beauty of those who helped her in her grief. She found that God can heal a broken heart because he healed hers, and in the healing process she found a new life and a continuing peace with God.

A mother knew she was dying. She wrote a poem about the indescribable faith and beauty of being able to accept the fact that her earthly life was ending, but she also knew she was being prepared to receive her final inheritance from God.

God and I

Step by step, he gently leads
And grants to me his sight,
We now walk closer, God and I
Through valleys into light.

His arms are strong—I feel his touch,
He tells me not to fear.

Giving God What You Are

We talk together, God and I
His voice is strangely clear.

He whispers of his nearness
To remind me of his Grace
But it took the pain and darkness
To see him face to face.

—Jo Ellen Crites
(unpublished work)

Grief is inevitable, but along with it comes the inevitable love of God. There will never be anything that will happen in your life that God can't handle. By accepting this understanding of God's power and wisdom, discouragement will lose some of its power in your life. You have already been subjected to many of life's uncertainties. Some of them have been overcome by merely adjusting to the situation, while others have been more traumatic and you have not been able to handle them in your own strength. In the secret realm that only you and God share, pour out those longings before him and he will understand.

You may look at others and wonder how they have been able to withstand the grief they've experienced, but they know God has placed his love and power in their lives during those difficult moments.

These trials are only to test your faith, to see whether or not it is strong and pure. It is being tested as fire tests gold and purifies it—and your faith is far more precious to God than mere gold; so if your faith remains strong after being tried in the test tube of fiery trials, it will bring you much praise and glory and honor on the day of his return (1 Peter 1:7).

8
Giving God What You Have

One night I heard a woman sing. She presented a thrilling sacred concert. I had been to many vocal concerts before and had enjoyed the beautiful voices. But when I walked away from this concert, I was not praising her, the woman, the talent, but I was praising God for having given the world a life such as this. God had allowed her to put words and melodies together that thrilled thousands of people. Her voice and the messages she sang caused audiences to hear things they already may have known about God, but hearing them sung in such a powerful way undoubtedly helped many who heard her music to never again look upon life in quite the same way.

One morning I heard a sermon. The longer I listened the more I realized I was in the presence of God. I was no longer aware of the people in the congregation. It was me before God, worshiping him. I left when the service was over. I was not praising the man, the sermon, but I was praising God for putting this man on the earth to help me and others worship and honor the King.

I sat reluctantly waiting for a meeting to begin. I glanced at the program and thought, *Oh no! They're starting with a worship time and I don't want to worship. I don't feel like worshiping. I'm tired and I want this meeting to be over.* A young man stepped to the front of the room. He sat on a table and began to talk. The first thing I noticed was his smile. He began telling a story from the Bible about a man who was blind and who heard about a man who could cause him to see. It was a story I had heard as a small child, but it had a different connotation this time. I saw myself in the story. I was participating.

After the speaker had finished, he had us bow our heads and close our eyes. He asked three questions: What are some things you do not see although you are not blind? Where are places you do not go although you can walk? What are some things you can say, but you do not use your voice to say? I had been negligent in all of these ways. My services as a Christian had been so small. I had been selfish with the physical blessings that were mine. Suddenly, someone was covering my eyes with a blindfold. The room was quiet. After a few minutes, I heard some movement in the room. Soon I felt someone removing my blindfold and whispering to me, "God loves you." I looked around, and there were others who still had blindfolds on. We hadn't been told what to do, but I instinctively walked over to someone and whispered, "God loves you." I gave him his sight by removing his blindfold. Then, since I had received my sight, I sat watching others receiving theirs.

I don't actually know what else went on that morning, but I left the room thanking God and praising him for using a man to show me how God can use a life, and how the man himself was willing to share the way God had chosen for him to share with other people.

These three events brought about a new dimension in my life. I had heard other musicians in the past, I had heard many sermons and many Bible stories told, but these three times were different. People were performing services, but I was seeing God. I was getting to know him better through

126

what he was doing through their lives. I wanted more than anything to know that I, too, had something to share, something that would tell others about Christ. But how would I start? How could I learn what it was that he wanted me to share, and how did he want me to go about sharing what I knew to be true about his life?

> Then he said to all, "Anyone who *wants* to follow me must put aside his own desires and conveniences and carry his cross with him every day and keep close to me! Whoever loses his life for my sake will save it, but whoever insists on keeping his life will lose it; and what profit is there in gaining the whole world when it means forfeiting one's self? (Luke 9:23-25). Author's italics.

Do you know something about Christ that would help another life if they knew it, too? Perhaps some person once told you about Jesus and what he could do for your life. You began studying, observing, experiencing, and everything you learned, saw, and felt, filled your life with good things.Your Christian life kept getting fuller and you came to the place where you could no longer keep all of it to yourself. You had to give it away to someone who would listen and hear, perhaps for the first time, about the promises of eternal life.

A man was going blind. Each morning he got up and washed the matter from his eyes. His sight was dim, but he was grateful for one more day with the sight that was left. He was able to continue his plowing and do the numerous daily chores, and yet he couldn't bring himself to tell his family his hurtful secret.

One morning he awoke. He washed his eyes. He was still in darkness as he had been many mornings, but this morning was different. He scrubbed his eyes again—continued darkness. He stumbled into the kitchen and told his family his secret. They gathered around him and hugged him. His family's assurance had seen him through his first sightless day.

The neighbors came to thresh his grain. The children did his farm chores. His wife brought him his meals. But the day came when other activities filled his children's days, the neighbors settled back into their own work, and his wife didn't come around as much as she had at first.

One morning at dawn he packed his belongings in a sack, and while all the others were asleep he stumbled out of the house and found his way to join the city beggars. He made acquaintance with other blind men and began to share a similar existence. They stood at the same city gate, begging, listening, learning to accept the loss of never being able to see again. Then he and the others heard about a man. He was making the deaf to hear, the crippled to walk and, miracles of miracles—the blind to see.

Jesus was the man who could give him his sight. He was the one who could gather up the remnants of the blind man's life and make something meaningful of it.

Be Willing to Give

You've heard about Jesus. You accepted all he had to offer you. Now, more than anything else you will want to help someone to see Christ the way you have come to see him, the way he's working through your life, and the way he can work through theirs. You want people to know that in him we "live and move and are!" (Acts 17:28). This requires something very unselfish from you. You are beginning the process of losing your life for Christ so that someone else can find eternal life.

How does a Christian get completely out and away from himself, lose himself from the old selfishness that devours and diminishes so many precious days? How can you keep from being captured by the world so completely that you are not

Giving God What You Have

willing to lose your life for Christ in order to find the abundant life the Bible talks about? How can you get out of your structured routine of paying bills, buying groceries, pursuing a hobby, being an active citizen of the community, in order to have time to tell and show other people what you've learned, and are continuing to learn, about God?

God tells you how. "Anyone who *wants* to follow me. . . ." God has made the acceptance of eternal life simple enough for anyone who will believe in it. He will take any life that *wants* to be used and he will use it. This willingness will put you into places you never thought possible, but you know God has put you there because your *want* is being stimulated by him. You've told him you want to follow him. When you begin doing service for God, he gives you the ability and the right motives for doing it. The people won't be seeing you, the person; they will be seeing God and what he can do for them, through your life.

If you're a new Christian and just beginning to see what Christ is doing through your life, you will want to share even that. If you have been a Christian for several years, you will want to let other people know how God has been with you and helped you through every situation, and how his words in the Bible have become living proof that what God promises he delivers. You know you have the promise of eternal life and that should be the first thing you will want to share. You already know that he walks through valleys as dark as death because he has walked with you. You know he gives peace because you've received it. You understand he listens to you pray because you have gone before him many times and he has heard you. You can no longer keep all of these wondrous acts of God to yourself.

If there were one word that could be used to prepare you to

share your life with others, it would be the word *willing*. I believe God chooses imperfect people who love him and are willing to give of themselves to do his work. When you tell God you're willing to do anything, he takes your feeble efforts and makes something useful from them. What kind of service does God accept? How large an act has to be performed before God notices it, before it can benefit anyone else?

A small boy was playing with his friends. While he was playing, one of his neighbors called to him and asked him if he would like to go see Jesus. He ran into his house to ask his mother if he could go. She knew it was close to mealtime, so she packed a lunch for him to take. When they reached the rest of the crowd, Jesus was already speaking. The boy got as close as he could. He wanted to get a glimpse of Jesus and hear his voice.

He had never heard anyone speak like this before. Jesus' voice was strong enough for all the thousands of people that were there. His voice was also soft enough that he seemed to be speaking to each person individually.

It was midafternoon before there was a break in what Jesus was saying. The boy got to his feet and stretched. He suddenly realized he was hungry. As he was spreading out his lunch, one of Jesus' followers came over to him and began talking with him. Soon Jesus' follower heard his name being called, so he left.

After the young boy had said his prayer of thanksgiving for his food, he saw approaching him the disciple who had talked with him just a few minutes before. He told the boy that Jesus wanted to see him and to bring his lunch along. The boy grabbed his lunch and hurried along with the disciple. Jesus asked the boy if he would be willing to share his lunch. The boy didn't question what Jesus asked but knew that if Jesus wanted his lunch, he wanted to share it with him.

Jesus took the five small loaves of bread and the two fish. He then thanked God for them. Then he began breaking them and distributing them to the crowd. Every time Jesus broke the bread or the fish, there seemed to be more. And when it was all over, the boy saw that his lunch, in the hands of Jesus, had fed a crowd of five thousand people.

Your life, in the hands of Jesus, can perform miracles. All Jesus had asked of the young boy was for him to share his lunch. That didn't seem like such a big thing, but have you ever wondered how it affected the boy's life after that? Jesus asked him to do this small thing, he responded without questioning, and he experienced a miracle. All Jesus asks you to share is what you have. Maybe you can't do certain things, but you can do the will of God. "It isn't sacrifices and offerings which you really want from your people. . . . But you have accepted the offer of my lifelong service" (Ps. 40:6). As you continue to progress in your Christian journey, you will see what else might be involved in working for God and what part of your life you still have not handed him. Your seeking indicates to God that you are willing to become involved in others' lives. You are losing your life for Christ. That becomes the true motive of your sharing. Nothing else is acceptable before God.

Christ becomes your Lord when you yield all you are to all he wants you to be. You should go before God at the beginning of each day and tell him you're handing your life over to him for that day. If he wants to use your hands, be ready. If he wants you to speak, yield to him. If he wants you to go somewhere, go. By releasing the hold you have on your life, God can begin working through you, and your life will multiply over and over in its effectiveness.

Giving God What You Are

I met a visitor in church one Sunday. I knew nothing about her except that she and her family had just moved to our community. She had a beautiful smile and was friendly. After we had exchanged the regular greetings, she asked me to stop by her house some day for coffee. She gave me her address, which I immediately recognized as being in the elite part of town. I dismissed her invitation for awhile, but one day she called me to come over for that cup of coffee, and the next day I drove to her house. It was as elegant as I had imagined it would be. I had no idea what we would have in common to talk about, but that proved to be no problem. Since we were both married, the natural course of conversation was our families. After we had gone through the preliminaries, this woman began sharing about her desires for her family. Her husband and children were not Christians. Her husband was much older than she, an intelligent man and a highly successful businessman. When his wife had talked with him about becoming a Christian, he told her matter-of-factly that there had never been anything he couldn't handle, therefore, he saw no need for God in his life. How burdened she became as she told me about this man she loved. I cried with her, and those tears we shed together that morning were to produce a lasting bond between us.

Two weeks later her husband had a stroke. I talked with her on the phone. She told me that he was to have an operation. Even if he survived, he would never be able to speak. We prayed. He lived through the operation, and he was able to speak. During his recovery, he told his wife that he had had an experience with God. I don't know what he was trying to convey when he told his wife about that encounter but I want to believe that he had a beginning of at least acknowledging that there was a God. Hopefully he would learn later that this God had extended his grace to him, and he would eventually give his life to God.

Before we moved from that city, my friend and I never did get up the courage to tell each other good-bye, but something happened that culminated my service to her family. She called and said that her daughter was interested in becoming a Christian and asked me if I would please talk with her. How I prayed before she came. We talked and then we held hands and prayed together, and I thanked God for that young life. She and her mother left the house, and I have never seen them again, although they are still a part of my life.

Jesus touched that woman's life and mine the first day we met. I didn't realize he could get so much started just by my accepting an invitation to have coffee with another person. I can't even think about what I would have missed had I allowed myself to feel inadequate to visit with that woman because of the differences in our social backgrounds. As she and I prayed together, her husband saw Christ and her daughter accepted him. What more could I ever ask to happen in my life?

The only thing that might be in the way of your being willing to put your entire life into God's hands is that you're too busy doing other things. Martha and Mary invited Jesus to have a meal with them. Martha was very busy in the kitchen, and she resented Mary not helping her. She came in and said, " 'Doesn't it seem unfair to you that my sister just sits here, while I do all the work?' . . . But the Lord said to her, 'Martha, dear friend, you are upset over all these details! There is really only one thing worth being concerned about. Mary has discovered it—and I won't take it away from her!' " (Luke 10:40-42).

Everything we do takes discipline. It is a busy world, there are many important things to do, but are we always doing the most important things, and if we are doing them, are we doing them for Christ? Are things—ambitions, meetings, social schedules—keeping you from being involved in things that are lasting?

I don't know anyone who can get much serious thinking done, especially about a matter such as this, in the midst of noise. Jesus found the solution for this. He retreated from the crowds. He went to the mountains. He got alone. It was then that he revived his spirit and communed with his Father. It's amazing what you can hear when it gets quiet. Perhaps you have had a longing to do more with your life. Can you think of a quiet place—a city park, a room in your house, a country road, a lake, the woods, a sanctuary where you can get away from your daily responsibilities and people, and talk with God? In the silence you can feel God's power when you are ready to listen to him. In that silence pray:

"God, I don't feel like I have that much to give you, but I'm willing. Please come into my life and let me know what I can do, in your strength, and I will do it. If you want me to continue doing what I'm doing now, I'm willing. If there is an area of my life I have not given to you, I'm willing. All I know is that if I am ever to get away from living my own life, I must offer myself up to you. Amen."

If you offer your lifelong service in this way, God will accept it. There is something unique about this "self" offering. Your daily work becomes a pleasure. Your life is not only an outward appearance to others, but your life becomes a gift; you accept it as that, and then you willingly give away the gift of life you have in Christ. You've seen other people sharing the joy of their salvation, and now you're ready to do the same thing.

134

Giving God What You Have
Some Who Have Given

Who are some of the most fulfilled people you know? They have something in common with each other—serving God according to their abilities. They have given up the trivialities of life, and instead they continually seek its purpose. They're wanting to live more abundantly. They are putting their faith and time into values that are going to last. They are learning to be at peace with themselves. They are seeing, helping, and giving. They are living for God in their daily circumstances. They are anticipating what God has for them to do. This growth is continuous, and they are reaching and achieving the stature to which Christ is calling them. All of this does not mean that they aren't working in adverse conditions, at times, but they are learning how to overcome them as they strive to be what God wants them to be.

You can read about people performing services, but until you see similar situations, they don't have as full an impact on you. Jesus taught people by example so that they could see what his teachings were all about. He not only told stories that people could relate to he also performed many services. One of the last services he performed in his earthly ministry was when he took the position of a servant before his disciples.

It was customary for the Jews to have their feet washed before they entered anyone's home. Since they walked along dusty streets and wore open sandals, their feet would get dirty. Before they entered any house, someone would meet them at the door with a basin of water and a towel. That person would remove the guest's sandals, rinse the dust from his feet, dry them, and then welcome him into the house. If there were a servant in that particular house he would do this service. If there were no servants, one of the children would do it. If there were no children, the host would do it.

Since the disciples were entering a borrowed room there were no servants, no children, and no appointed host. As they came into the room they probably noticed the customary basin of water and towel at the door and wondered whose job it was to perform this service. No one seemed to want to do it, so they went into the room with dirty feet. As they were seated around the table, they began arguing among themselves as to which one of them was the most important. The arguing could possibly have started because no one had volunteered to act as host and wash their feet as they came into the room. As they were arguing, Jesus got up from the table without saying anything. He took the basin and towel and began going around the table washing the disciples' feet. "Do you understand what I was doing? You call me 'Master' and 'Lord,' and you do well to say it, for it is true. And since I, the Lord and Teacher, have washed your feet, you ought to wash each other's feet. I have given you an example to follow: do as I have done to you" (John 13:12-15).

If Jesus, who knew it would be just a few hours before he would be crucified, could become a servant at that time, then there can be no task too small or too undesirable for anyone to accept from him.

What Do You Have to Give?

Your life is going to touch someone else's life within the next twenty-four hours. You are going to see people who are dirty, sophisticated, renowned, young, old, ambitious, self-centered, friendly, unfriendly, self-conscious, timid. You will not have to wait until you get the daily newspaper to see how people like these are suffering, how children are being mistreated, or how older people are trying to cope with loneliness. These are people who have been created by God, just like you. They need help. They need you. You cannot alleviate all the suffering, but you can help some.

When you became a Christian, it was more than a transaction between you and God. You now will want to share what life can be with God. No person can tell you what you're to do. Somehow you must evaluate your life honestly, hiding nothing from yourself or from God. You must look at your life at face value. If you have to, look in the mirror, confront yourself honestly, and say, "Am I never to do anything for God except what *I* want to do?" That kind of service entails getting completely away from the selfish nature that will plague you, as a Christian, for the rest of your life.

Where do you start? What do you have to give? Ask God. There may be times when he will ask you to do the most simple things, but you might ignore what he is telling you because you fail to see the significance of what he is asking.

Consider the simple thing that Naaman, the commander-in-chief of his king's army, was asked to do. He was a leper. He heard that the prophet Elisha could heal him. The king insisted that Naaman go to Elisha and be healed. Elisha told Naaman that in order to be cured of his leprosy, he was to go wash himself in the Jordan River seven times. But this made Naaman mad. He thought the cure could be done in a different way, and besides, the Jordan River was a very dirty river. Then one of his officers said, "If the prophet had told you to do some great thing, wouldn't you have done it? So you should certainly obey him when he says simply to go and wash and be cured" (2 Kings 5:13). Naaman accepted this suggestion and went immediately to the Jordan River. He dipped himself in it seven times, and he was healed. All he needed to do to be healed was to do specifically what he was asked to do.

Giving God What You Are

God will be asking you to do certain things. First, there may be things he will want you to do to prepare yourself for service. This should not be overlooked when you are asking God how he can use your life. After the necessary preparations have been made and the time is right, God will begin using you in a way you never thought possible. With him living through you, you will have such an abundance of potential sharing that you will be unable to keep from giving this God that you love the praise, the adoration, and the declaration of your highest honor. There is no earthly force that will keep you from putting into motion all there is to share about God.

Two Christian men felt they had to go talk with an elderly man who had been attending their church. The man was not a Christian. The wife of one of the men tried to discourage them from going."He may stop coming to church if you say the wrong thing." But she did not hinder the enthusiasm of the two men. They drove to the man's house and prayed before they got out of the car. When they knocked on the door, the man's wife opened it. She smiled and said, "I'm glad you came. We were waiting for you."

Years ago a neighbor had been confined to her bed for six weeks with pneumonia. Her bedroom was upstairs and she did not have access to a telephone. After six weeks the doctor allowed her to get out of bed and go downstairs. On her first day up, the phone rang. Her husband answered it and said, "One of your friends is on the phone." She picked up the telephone. There was no voice on the other end of the line, but for several moments she listened to the most beautiful strains of music being played on her friend's violin. After the song was over, the caller placed the receiver on the hook. No words were needed in the joyful silence that followed.

A young man leaves his house early each morning to help a wife get her crippled husband out of bed.

Giving God What You Have

A young woman works in a nursing home. As she walks by each person, she gently touches their faces or places her arms around their shoulders and smiles.

A mentally deficient man hands out bulletins at church each Sunday. He shakes hands with everyone that comes.

A doctor's family travels to Africa on vacation, only the vacation is spent healing the sick bodies of those living there.

These people saw needs of other people. They knew what a gentle touch, a smile, a handshake could do because they had felt similar needs in their own lives. They knew the importance of listening and talking with others because they had wanted to do the same. They were being moved with compassion just as Jesus was moved each time he was in a crowd.

When I was a child I was always anxious to hear the 4:00 whistle because this alerted me that mother would be on her way home from work. Many times I'd be in the front yard and would see her walking down the gravel road. But one day it was different. I was standing as usual, waiting for her. It was an extremely hot summer day. I could see mother coming, but I didn't run to her immediately. I found myself looking at her face. She looked tired, as I'm sure she had looked many times before, but that was the first time I can remember noticing it. She was tired and I wanted to do something to help her so she wouldn't have to work so hard. I believe that was my first experience of feeling such strong compassion for anyone.

Jesus saw people who were sick, tormented, hated, crippled, unhappy, evil, and he was continually moved with compassion. You can read at many places in the Scriptures about how Jesus' entire ministry was performed out of a heart of compassion. Then you see other people exemplifying his example, and you know you must adopt this level of love in your life if you are ever to share what you know to be true about Jesus.

It is evident by the way people are allowing their lives to be

Giving God What You Are

used by God that they have access to two things: God's love that guides them into awareness and concern, and enough time to see things that need to be done and to do them.

You may be at a crucial point in your Christian life. Perhaps you are not satisfied to live out the rest of your life in your present spiritual state, and wish to give yourself more fully to God. You should make an appeal before God, with humility, with all the knowledge you have about him, and ask him if there is still a part of your life that you haven't given to him. You must acknowledge to God a desire that will not be quieted until everything you are has been released to him.

It is difficult to relinquish your life for spiritual purposes when your're living in the world and being affected by its powerful, constant influences. So, for a moment, remove yourself from the world—retreat from it. Standing at this vantage point, you will see a world that brings distinction to the wealthy and ignores the poor, that gives honor to those who succeed but has nothing to give to those who try. You will see people who strive for worldwide recognition but don't know their neighbor, who seek continuous pleasures but never stop to visit the lonely, who spend millions on projects, organizations, and objects that will eventually disappear, but do not understand the eternal value of a soul.

Now step back into the world. You have seen the intensities of man's selfish drives—his hates, his misplaced priorities, and his injustices. God has seen all of these from the beginning of the world, and he still, after all of this time, continues to be moved with compassion. These are his people, a part of his creation. To help these people, to share with them, you are simply asked to go before God, offer your lifelong service to him, and he will accept it!

Postscript

God has walked close by me the past three years as I have written this book. There have been mornings that I wouldn't spend nearly enough time with God before I started to write, and at those times my work would not be its best. Instead of taking so much time asking him how he wanted this book to be written, he taught me as we went along that the writing, although important, was not to come before him. Not only in my writing but in every hour of my life, in every activity of each day, none of these things were to come before him. This is not a truth that comes from a selfish God. It is a truth for living, and it is the only way that I can live at peace in a world that struggles daily for peace but cannot find it because it doesn't understand God's peace.

Through this finished work, I have discovered that there is no part of my life that God isn't interested in. He wants to have it all, to perfect it all. I have struggled, but in struggling I have gained more insight into God's patience. I have been discouraged, but in that discouragement I have developed hope for better days. I have felt completly undone and lost in the very thing God was asking me to do, but he continued to walk with me in my journey.

As God and I went along, he caused me to look closely at my life. Some of the things that were drawn from my memory made me ashamed, others made me grateful. But whatever I discovered, God kept saying, "I still love you."

In the past year I have tried to complete this book, but every time I thought I had finished it something else would happen in my life. I would hear another beautiful song about God and his love, I would meet another person, I would read another book, I would have another experience which would cause me to know God in still another way—I had to share those things with you, also.

Now I know there can never be a complete ending to this book. Jesus' own story has never ended. His story, his life, will always continue because it involves eternity. It is this belief that you and I have personally claimed, that we will be in God's presence in everything that happens to us in this world. In the same faith with which we accepted God into our lives, we have been assured that there is life after death. For every Christian, that means that even when we leave this earth we will continue to live in the presence of God throughout eternity.

I know of nothing else to share with you except to say with the apostle Paul:"I don't mean to say I'm perfect, I haven't learned all I should even yet, but I keep working toward that day when I will finally be all that Christ saved me for and wants me to be" (Phil. 3:12).